First published in 2017 by Barrallier Books Pty Ltd,
trading as Echo Books

Registered Office: 35-37 Gordon Avenue, West Geelong, Victoria 3220, Australia.

www.echobooks.com.au

National Library of Australia Cataloguing-in-Publication entry.

Creator: Fielding, Marcus, compiler.

Title: Jack Bell's War : The remarkable story of an Australian airman and POW in North Africa, Italy and Germany/MarcusFielding.

IISBN: 9780648074595 (hardback)

Subjects: Bell, Jack. World War, 1939-1945—Aerial operations, Australian.

World War, 1939-1945—Prisoners and prisons, Australian—Biography.

Prisoners of war—Australia—Biography.

World War, 1939-1945—Personal narratives, Australian.

Australia—History—20th century.

Book layout and design by Peter Gamble, Canberra.
Set in Garamond Premier Pro Display, 12/17 and Minerva Antiqua.

www.echobooks.com.au

JACK BELL'S WAR

The remarkable story of an Australian airman and POW in North Africa, Italy and Germany

Marcus Fielding

ECHO BOOKS

TABLE OF CONTENTS

FOREWORD

Major General David McLachlan, AO
Former State President of the Victorian Branch of the Returned and
Services League of Australia

There are many men and women in our Australian community who are truly inspirational but we don't always have the insight into their lives to understand what makes them so.

John Robert Bell, known as Jack, is a good example. To meet him today, he is a fine upstanding, gentleman in the true sense of the word who you would assess as being in his middle eighties. Always immaculately dressed, he is sprightly in step and lively in conversation. A truly inspirational figure. He served in the Royal Australian Air Force during the Second World War and flew as aircrew. The proverb 'A picture tells a thousand words' couldn't be further from the truth when applied to Jack Bell.

Marcus Fielding, in the following chapters of his biography, beautifully sets out why Jack is one of a very special group of men in our society. One who volunteered to serve his nation, travelled to the other side of the world to do so, was shot down in flight, severely wounded and captured. He was not only interned by the Germans but passed to the Italians and then go back to German control before the war ended. Much of Marcus' writing centres on Jack's time as a POW in Campo 57 and Stalag IV-B.

It is amazing to think of how Jack must have felt having survived the crash of his Bristol Bombay, being severely wounded and initially ending up in a German medical facility where the surgeon had been a Harley Street specialist before the war began. How lucky are we as Australians that this was so and this icon was to eventually return home.

Jack Bell arrived back in Australia in September 1945 and returned to his previous occupation at D & W Murray Ltd in Brisbane. He eventually moved to Melbourne, where he married and still lives today.

It took Jack some 40 years to write about his war experiences, something I think he regrets. Like so many Second World War Veterans, Jack's early encounter with the Returned & Services League was not what it should have been.

He eventually became a member in Victoria and he has been of tremendous assistance in various appeals to assist our veterans. When you speak with him today he stresses the importance of communication particularly for those returning from recent conflict. His message to those young men and woman is to talk to your mates and seek help early if you need it.

In December this year Jack Bell will turn 100 years of age. On behalf of all who will read this biography I thank Marcus for his work in allowing us to share such insight into the life of a truly remarkable Australian.

David McLachlan AO

Jack Bell–My Story

My story is being published thanks to the Camberwell RSL. Some months ago a member of the Committee, Bill Upfield, asked if he could borrow my story written some thirty years ago. Unbeknown to me he submitted the story to the RSL committee who accepted the responsibility to publish. Dolores and I were overcome at such a decision, our sincerest thanks to them.

A number of my ex-POW friends had in the past published their stories from time to time, some successful but most not. To purchase 2000 books, sell two to three hundred and then have the rest left stored in the garage? I decided not for me.

Our daughter, Sandra, came to see me mid-1987 and said 'Dad, Mum knows nothing of your story nor do I and neither will your grandchildren. Can you write down your recollections of your period as a POW.' This took me three years to do so—the first two years I could only write my name and date on the top of a page—it was just so hard to let the memories back in. A group of about fifteen of us used to meet regularly on the east coast for holidays telling our wives about the funny things that happened as POWs but hiding the unpleasant side.

Then in 1990 I started to write whilst on holidays on the Gold Coast and once started the words flowed and flowed. Once I had written about the experiences I was also able to talk to people outside of my wartime mates and now I am a willing speaker at schools and clubs, telling my story. Our very good friend, Lloyd Morris, typed it out for me and made five copies one of which I gave to Lloyd and the others to Sandra for her family.

During the next 25 to 30 years I received numerous accounts of events that happened during our imprisonment and I acknowledge the wonderful help I have received. My thanks to Tom Roberts, author of *Wingless* which is a collection of information of all RAAF POWs in all theatres of war (approximately 2000).

I have intense feelings for the boys coming back from the recent Iraq and Afghanistan conflicts over the past 10 or so years. I strongly believe that medicines do much to help but we found sharing our stories with mates and helping each other went a long way to bring us back to some sort of normality. My loving wife of 63 years had to suffer nightmares, me thrashing about in my sleep, sometimes hitting her not knowing I had done so. Holding me and helping me back to reality. Even in my twilight years at times these bogies come.

To the reader of this book I say understand and give all you can to support those lads. Give yourself and try to understand how difficult it is for those young men to come back to our world.

Marcus Fielding has spent many hours with me and untold hours checking my story with official records dating back most of my 100 years of life. Thank you so much and I am sure you will get the praise you deserve in providing my story so wonderfully well.

David McLachlan, thank you for the very kind words written in your foreword.

Sharing with my pals from Stalag IV-B our problems undoubtedly helped us to fit back into normal life. Dolores and I have for many years given our time to helping those in need. We ask to generously give your time to help—it costs nothing to give your time but it is of great help to those in need.

My time spent among thousands of prisoners of at least 30 nationalities has helped me to be respectful, tolerant and compassionate towards our fellow man.

Thank you,

Jack Bell

INTRODUCTION

On 20 December 2017 Jack Bell celebrated his 100th birthday; a great achievement for any person but very special when that person was seriously wounded in the Second World War and survived over three years in Italian and German Prisoner of War camps.

Even at this senior age Jack maintains his parade ground posture, dresses smartly and has a razor sharp mind. He looks much younger than he is—and when he relays that he fought in the Second World War the first reaction is usually one of disbelief.

Jack's experiences as an airman and Prisoner of War (POW) in the Second World War make a remarkable story. He enlisted in the Royal Australian Air Force at age 22. He saw active service in North Africa during one of the great Allied offensives. His aircraft was shot down by the Germans and he was badly wounded. After recovering in hospital and surviving for over three years in three POW camps he was liberated by the Russians. When Jack was demobilised in early 1946 he had just turned 28—another seven decades of his life still lay ahead of him.

This book was written as a tribute to Jack's service to the nation and the community. It was produced in partnership with the Camberwell City Sub-Branch of the Returned and Services League of Australia.

I would like to acknowledge their financial and moral support in producing this book. It drew material from his personal files, interviews, archives and open sources. I would like to thank Jack and his family for their support in producing this book. While all due care has been taken to research the material for this book any errors remain mine.

Marcus Fielding

The Boys from Hut 36B

Strolling in group beneath Grafton's Jacaranda trees onlookers would have little idea on what might have brought this collection of older gentlemen together. Perhaps high school? Perhaps an interest in golf? But within the group they knew that it was surviving together those long cold and hungry months in Hut 36B at Stalag IV-B.

Packed tight and huddled together for warmth, they made and shared what little food they had; they nursed each other through sickness, they jollied each other up when morale was low, and, over time, they become brothers.

Decades later they would come together for a few days to celebrate their friendship and their lives—lived to the fullest in honour of those who did not come back. News was swapped but invariably the conversation would always turn back to reminisces about their time in the camp.

No one but them would ever really appreciate their thoughts and feelings. Wives and children might develop some level of understanding, but the experience was life-changing for them and more often than not supressed for decades. Some had not survived the peacetime journey and fallen victim to alcohol, violence or suicide. Others did survive and only as they reached their senior years encouraged to talk and write.

The gatherings were cathartic—the more they talked the more they could put their experiences into perspective. Over time others came to understand and appreciate their experiences and now those that remain are venerated.

Few people alive today have a first-hand experience of the Second World War. The scale of the event and the impact that it had can scarcely be comprehended by those who were not there. When the veterans of that horrible time gather on Anzac Day and other occasions we must draw on their service and sacrifice and ensure that we don't forget.

Jack with his some of his Hut 36B mates in the late 1980s
Back row (L to R): Sandy Mostran, Sandy Jones, Dick Osborn, Frank Beste and Jack Bell
Front row (L to R) Jock Watson, Alec Richardson and Gus Officer

The Road to War

On a balmy day in the week before Christmas Day the Bell family was blessed with the birth of their third child. Robert (Bert) and Caroline (Carrie) had married in April 1914 and moved into a house in Elizabeth Street in Toowong. Laurie was born in that house on 23 January 1915 and Thelma on 8 June 1916.

John Robert Bell was brought into the world on 20 December 1917 at ten past five in the afternoon with Nurse Abbott attending as mid-wife. Bert wanted to name John after his father and Carrie wanted to name him Jack after Jack Moffatt—a friend of the family. Bert won the contest on the birth certificate but Carrie consistently referred to John as Jack. After about ten years Carrie won out and ever since everyone—including Bert—calls him 'Jack'. So, from now on our story will be about Jack.

Not long afterwards the family moved into 82 Church Street in Toowong. Located a couple of hundred metres from the Brisbane River the Bell family would remain in this house for the next 23 years and be joined by another son, Ronald, in February 1921. Jack recalls this family event and visiting his mother and brand new brother in the front bedroom of their home.

When the Prince of Wales visited Australia in 1920 Jack has memories of his father taking the family to the railway bridge at the top of the street and them looking down at the Prince standing on the back platform of the royal carriage as it passed.

Jack started school at the Toowong State School in 1923 and recalls his first teacher Mr Hopkins who was an expert in detecting misdemeanours and 'correcting' them with the accurate throw of a blackboard eraser or stick of chalk. Jack also recalls the school principal—a stickler for discipline—rushing down off the verandah to grab one of the 'big boys' by the arm and giving him six cuts across the backside in front of all the other students.

School holidays were usually spent at the family's seaside cottage at Sandgate. Bert and Carrie bought the beachfront land at 550 Flinders Parade for five pounds, and Bert pre-cut the entire house for 100 pounds. With Bert's friend and plumber Jack Moffat a busy few days saw the cottage erected and ready to be enjoyed. Jack remembers spending many an enjoyable holiday around Sandgate—playing with friends, swimming, boating and catching, cleaning and eating fish.

Toowong State School Grade 1 1923

550 Flinders Parade, Sandgate

Bert commuted from the cottage to and from work during the holidays in the family's model T Ford.

In February 1932 Jack started at Brisbane Boys College where academic studies seemed to take second place to playing sport—cricket, rugby union and cross-country running. But recognising the need to get good grades Jack applied himself and passed the public exam at the

The Bell Family's 1921 Model T Ford with Laurie, Thelma, Jack and Ronald

end of 1933 at age 15. He took the exam for the Junior Public Certificate at the University of Queensland and passed English, English history, geography, arithmetic, algebra, geometry and chemistry. Jack got a first class pass in physics.

After finishing school Jack started to look for work. The Depression was over but there were still a lot of people unemployed. After several weeks of walking into business offices and asking for work Jack began to become a bit despondent. Arriving home one day his mother told him to head back into town where a friend had advised there might be an opening. After waiting in line with 10 other boys Jack met with Mr Petersen at D.&W. Murray Ltd—a men's and boy's clothing warehouse on Elizabeth Street. When he got home Jack's mother informed him that he had to go back the next morning for another interview. A procession of boys marched in and out of the office and after Jack's turn he was brusquely told to 'stand over there'. A group of five boys were then taken upstairs and introduced to their new boss and the other staff members. The boys were then all put to work immediately and Jack not expecting this went the rest of the day with only a milkshake for lunch. He returned home exhausted but now luckily a member of the workforce. Jack's hours were long and the workload was relentless but at least he was earning an income. After three months he was made a permanent employee.

In November 1933 Bert took Jack and Laurie to the 'Gabba' to watch a Sheffield Shield match of cricket between New South Wales and Queensland. Jack Fingleton and Bill Brown opened the batting for New South Wales and after a solid start Fingleton was dismissed. Don Bradman came in at number three and proceeded to score 200 runs in 184 minutes—just over three hours! It was the first of several opportunities that Jack would have to marvel at Bradman's skill with the bat.

When Jack turned 18 in December 1935 he and his mate Sam Maxwell joined the Militia. They became members of the 14th Field Battery,

5th Field Artillery Brigade, Royal Australian Artillery. They learned to ride and drive horses as well as the drill requirements to operate the 18 pounder field guns. Jack then specialised as a gun layer on the 25 pounder field gun-howitzer and was promoted to Bombardier (Corporal equivalent).

A 25 pounder field gun-howitzer firing at night

Life over the next few years became a happy blend of work, playing cricket and rugby, swimming, socialising, surfing at the Maroochydore Surf Life Saving Club and enjoying his youth. When Jack turned 21 he was promoted to under manager of workwear and with that pay increase thought life was pretty good.

But in 1939 the storm clouds of war began to gather over Europe and in September Germany invaded Poland. Following a declaration of war by both Great Britain and France, the Australian Prime Minister Robert Menzies announced that Australia was also at war with Germany.

As war fever struck the nation Jack's militia unit went our bush for another exercise. During camp Jack reflected on how accurate they had become in firing artillery and then realised that the enemy might be

Jack Bell 1938

equally proficient. He then returned home and applying the logic that he would be harder to hit as a moving target decided to put his name down to join the Air Force. Later, he would prophetically realise that harder does not mean impossible.

In May 1940 as the phony war came to an end in Europe, Jack was called in to the Royal Australian Air Force enlistment office. Unfortunately the recruiting office was directly opposite D.&W. Murray Ltd so as he walked across the street his workmates encouraged him with calls of 'you'll be sorry'. Like thousands of others Jack signed up for 'the duration of the war and a period of twelve months thereafter.'

Jack wanted to be a pilot but was enlisted on 24 May 1940 as a Wireless Operator/Air Gunner under the Empire Air Training Scheme. His intake group was sent by train to Sydney where they were split into different training groups; the Wireless Operators then went on the train to Ballarat.

Unsurprisingly, Ballarat was cold, wet and miserable in late May. The weather matched the mood. Accommodated in basic galvanised iron covered buildings at the showgrounds the group was inducted into the RAAF and issued with their uniforms—no more than blue overalls and boots. Square bashing was the order of the first few weeks until the formal course in wireless and Morse code could commence. Colds and flus ran riot as well as other shared ailments from first living as a group. Time off from training was spent playing sport and socialising in town. The Wireless Operator Training course finished at the end of November 1940.

EMPIRE AIR TRAINING SCHEME

At the outbreak of the Second World War the British government realised it did not have adequate resources to maintain the Royal Air Force (RAF) in the impending air war in Europe. While British factories could rapidly increase their aircraft production, there was no guaranteed supply of trained aircrew. Pre-war plans had identified a need for 50,000 aircrew annually, but Britain could only supply 22,000.

To overcome this problem, the British government put forward a plan to its dominions to jointly establish a pool of trained aircrew who could then serve with the RAF. In Australia the proposal was accepted by the War Cabinet and a contingent was sent to a conference in Ottawa, in Canada, to discuss the proposal. After several weeks of negotiations, an agreement was signed on 17 December 1939 which would last for three years. The scheme was known in Australia as the Empire Air Training Scheme (EATS).

Under the Scheme 50,000 aircrew would be trained annually, each dominion would conduct its own elementary training; advanced training would be conducted in Canada because of its closeness to the British aircraft factories and the war zone. From November 1940, some training was also conducted in Rhodesia (now Zimbabwe).

Australia undertook to provide 28,000 aircrew over three years, which represented 36% of the total number of proposed aircrew. The first basic flying course started on 29 April 1940, when training began simultaneously in all participating countries. The first Australian contingent embarked for Canada on 14 November 1940. The following Royal Australian Air Force (RAAF) schools were established across Australia to support EATS:

- Initial Training
- Elementary Flying Training
- Service Flying Training
- Air Navigation
- Air Observer
- Bombing and Gunnery
- Wireless/Air Gunnery

Under Article XV of the agreement, it was proposed that each country's aircrew would serve in distinct national squadrons once they arrived in Britain. Eventually there were 17 Article XV RAAF squadrons, these being numbered 450–467 (but with No. 465 formed). Four of these units were in Fighter Command, seven in Bomber Command, and one in Coastal Command. Another five were also formed in the Middle East. However, despite Article XV, the bulk of Australian aircrew served with RAF squadrons and not with a designated Australian squadron.

The agreement was renewed for an additional two years in March 1943, although by then it was evident that the RAF already had a large surplus of aircrew. Throughout 1944 Australia's contribution to the scheme was wound back, at Britain's instigation, and the scheme effectively ended in October 1944, although it was not formally suspended until 31 March 1945. By this time, over 37,000 Australian airmen had been trained as part of the scheme.

WIRELESS OPERATOR/AIR GUNNER

The role of a Wireless Operator/Air Gunner was to send and receive wireless signals during the flight, assisting the Observer with triangulation fixes to aid navigation when necessary and, if attacked, to use the defensive machine gun armament of the bomber to fight off enemy aircraft. In the early stages of the war usually an enlisted man, he could hold any rank from Aircraftman 2nd Class upwards but was most often a Sergeant.

In the Royal Australian Air Force (RAAF) a Wireless Operator/Air Gunner wore a single-winged aircrew brevet with a wreath containing the letters 'AG' on his tunic, above his left breast pocket denoting his trade specialization and a cloth arm patch featuring a closed fist holding lightning bolts.

The Air Gunner's Badge

Sergeant Jack Robert Bell

The group was then sent to Evans Head in northern New South Wales for a four week course in gunnery. As Jack was already familiar with the basic action of the Lewis gun from his time in the Militia he quickly picked up the training on the Vickers machine gun. The greatest challenge was judging relative speed between two moving objects. Jack graduated from the Air Gunnery Course on 14 December 1940 and as was the norm promoted to Sergeant soon afterwards. He was just 23 years old and about to be sent to war.

After a short period of pre-embarkation leave with family and friends Jack travelled by train to Sydney. Sporting their hard earned

An aerial photograph of the No.1 Bombing and Gunnery School and No.1 Air Observers School, Evans Head, NSW

Graduation from 2nd EATS Gunnery School at Evans Head
14 December 1940

qualification badges and rank chevrons and finally in full uniform the group looked smart and keen to join the war. They embarked onto the *Aquitania* and sailed from Sydney on 4 February 1941 bound for Bombay.

On board the *Aquitania* officers occupied the upper decks and sergeants lower down, but the trip was uneventful and Jack rated the food as 'excellent'. During the voyage he met up with a lot of his old school mates.

After arriving in Bombay the group was encamped for a month at the Deolali Transit Camp—in the hills above Bombay. The Camp was notorious for its unpleasant environment and the boredom of soldiers that passed through it. Its name is the origin of the phrase 'gone doolally', a phrase meaning to 'lose one's mind. At the time the British Army unit at the Camp was The King's Own. Jack and his compatriots were less than impressed by the arrogance and racism of the British towards the Indian soldiers who they despised and took to with their swagger sticks for the slightest provocation. The Australians protested against this treatment but were dismissed as mere colonials. Nevertheless, the Indian soldiers noticed that their cause was being felt and so they looked after the Australians during their visit. Jack lamented that he would see a very similar attitude displayed by the British towards the 'Gypos' in Egypt.

The group's original destination was England but due to losses and shortages of air crews they were redirected to the Middle East theatre of operations. From Bombay Jack travelled on the *Windsor Castle* to Port Said in Egypt. The officer in charge of the embarked troops for this voyage was Frank Fisher who would later found Trans Australia Airlines. Two of Jack's mates smuggled a monkey out of India and managed to get him into Egypt where he later became a unit mascot.

AQUITANIA

The *Aquitania* was a Cunard Line ocean liner designed by Leonard Peskett and built by John Brown & Company in Clydebank, Scotland. She was launched on 21 April 1913 and sailed on her maiden voyage to New York on 30 May 1914. *Aquitania* was the third in Cunard Line's "grand trio" of express liners, preceded by RMS *Mauretania* and RMS *Lusitania*, and was the last surviving four-funnelled ocean liner. In her 36 years of service, *Aquitania* survived military duty in both world wars and was returned to passenger service after each.

Aquitania, with a normal troop capacity of 7,400, was among the select group of large, fast former passenger ships capable of sailing independently without escort transporting large numbers of troops that were assigned worldwide as needed. These ships, often termed "Monsters" until London requested the term be dropped, were *Aquitania*, *Queen Mary*, *Queen Elizabeth*, *Mauretania*, *Île de France* and *Nieuw Amsterdam* with "lesser monsters" being other large ex liners capable of independent sailing with large troop capacity that accounted for much of the troop capacity and deployment, particularly in the early days of the war.

Aquitania's initial troop transport operation during the Second World War was bringing Canadian troops to England in November 1939. Meanwhile, a massive transport of Australian and New Zealand troops to Suez and North Africa, with possible diversion to the United Kingdom if events required, was in planning with the numbered convoys to be designated as "US" with the large Atlantic liners assigned a role.

By 1941 the troop transport system was functioning efficiently and from 2 to 4 February troops embarked onto *Queen Mary* and *Aquitania* in Sydney. On 1 February

1941 *Nieuw Amsterdam* carrying New Zealand troops had departed Wellington and *Mauretania* was in Melbourne taking her troops on board.

Queen Mary, with nearly 6,000 troops on board, and *Aquitania* departed Sydney on 4 February 1941 and joined up with *Nieuw Amsterdam* off Sydney Heads. They headed for Melbourne, escorted by HMAS *Hobart*. They met *Mauretania* on 6 February 1941 in Bass Strait and headed for Fremantle.

Convoy US9 arrived in Fremantle on 9 February 1941 and departed westward on 12 February 1941, escorted by HMAS *Canberra*. The troops on board *Queen Mary* thought they were heading for the Middle East, but a few days out of Fremantle, *Queen Mary*, which was at the head of the convoy, swung around behind the other ships, came up alongside them again for a farewell pass and then turned for Singapore. The other three troopships headed for Bombay, where they arrived on 22 February 1941.

RMS Aquitania

EATS Courses 1 and 2 arrive in Sydney 2 February 1941

The Deolali Transit Camp

'Buzz' (right) the No. 3 Squadron RAAF Mascot

NORTH AFRICAN CAMPAIGN

The North African Campaign of the Second World War took place in North Africa from 10 June 1940 to 13 May 1943. It included campaigns fought in the Libyan and Egyptian deserts (Western Desert Campaign, also known as the Desert War) and in Morocco and Algeria (Operation Torch) and Tunisia (Tunisia Campaign).

The campaign was fought between the Allies and Axis powers, many of whom had colonial interests in Africa dating from the late 19th century. The Allied war effort was dominated by the British Commonwealth and exiles from German-occupied Europe. The United States entered the war in December 1941 and began direct military assistance in North Africa on 11 May 1942.

Fighting in North Africa started with the Italian declaration of war on 10 June 1940. On 14 June, the British Army's 11th Hussars crossed the border from Egypt into Libya and captured the Italian Fort Capuzzo. This was followed by an Italian counter-offensive into Egypt and the capture of Sidi Barrani in September 1940 and again in December 1940 following a British Commonwealth counteroffensive, Operation Compass. During Operation Compass, the Italian 10th Army was destroyed and the German Afrika Korps - commanded by Erwin Rommel, who later became known as 'The Desert Fox' - was dispatched to North Africa in February 1941.

Rommel's orders were to reinforce the Italians and block Allied attempts to drive them out of the region. However, the initial commitment of only one panzer division and subsequently, no more than two panzer and one motorized divisions, indicated the limited extent of German involvement and commitment in this theatre of operations. The bulk of the reinforcements were Italian and therefore it was up to the Italians to do the bulk of the fighting. The forward Allied force - now named XIII Corps - adopted a defensive posture and over the coming months was built up, before having most of its veteran forces redeployed to Greece. In addition, the 7th Armoured Division was withdrawn to the Nile delta. The veteran forces were replaced by inexperienced forces, ill-equipped to face German armour.

Although Rommel had been ordered to simply hold the line, an armoured reconnaissance soon became a full-fledged offensive from El Agheila in March 1941. In March–April 1941, the Allied forces were forced back and leading general officers captured. The Australian 9th Infantry Division fell back to the fortress port of Tobruk, and the remaining British and Commonwealth forces withdrew a further 100 mi (160 km) east to the Libyan–Egyptian border. With Tobruk under siege from the main Italian-German force, a small battlegroup continued to press eastwards. Capturing Fort Capuzzo and Bardia in passing, it then advanced into Egypt, and by the end of

April had taken Sollum and the tactically important Halfaya Pass. Rommel garrisoned these positions, reinforcing the battle-group and ordering it onto the defensive.

Though isolated by land, Tobruk's garrison continued to receive supplies and replacements, delivered by the Royal Navy at night. Rommel's forces did not have the strength or training to take the fortress. This created a supply problem for his forward units. His front-line positions at Sollum were at the end of an extended supply chain that stretched back to Tripoli and had to bypass the coast road at Tobruk. Further, he was constantly threatened by a breakout of the British forces at Tobruk. Without Tobruk in Axis hands, further advances into Egypt were impractical.

The Allies soon launched a small-scale counter-attack called Operation Brevity. This was an attempt to push the Axis forces off the key passes at the border, which gained some initial success, but the advanced position could not be held. Brevity was then followed up by a much larger-scale offensive, Operation Battleaxe. Intended to relieve the siege at Tobruk, this operation also failed.

Following the failure of Operation Battleaxe, Archibald Wavell was relieved of command and replaced by Claude Auchinleck. The Western Desert Force was reinforced with a second corps, XXX Corps, with the two corps forming the Eighth Army. Eighth Army was made up of army forces from the Commonwealth nations, including the British Army, the Australian Army, the British Indian Army, the New Zealand Army, the South African Army, and the Sudan Defence Force. There was also a brigade of Free French under Marie-Pierre Koenig. The new formation launched a new offensive, Operation Crusader, in November 1941. After a see-saw battle, the 70th Division garrisoning Tobruk was relieved and the Axis forces were forced to fall back. By January 1942, the front line was again at El Agheila.

After receiving supplies and reinforcements from Tripoli, the Axis attacked again, defeating the Allies at Gazala in June 1942 and capturing Tobruk. The Axis forces drove the Eighth Army back over the Egyptian border, but their advance was stopped in July 1942 only 90 mi (140 km) from Alexandria in the First Battle of El Alamein.

General Auchinleck, although he had checked Rommel's advance at the First Battle of El Alamein, was replaced by General Harold Alexander. Lieutenant-General William Gott was promoted from XIII Corps commander to take command of the entire Eighth Army, but he was killed when his aircraft was intercepted and shot down over Egypt. He was replaced by Lieutenant-General Bernard Montgomery.

At the end of June 1942, the Axis forces made a second attempt to break through the Allied defences at El Alamein at Alam Halfa, but were unsuccessful. After a lengthy period of build-up and training, the Eighth Army launched a major offensive, decisively defeating the Italian-German army during the Second Battle of El Alamein in late October 1942, driving the Axis forces westward and capturing Tripoli in mid-January 1943.

By February 1943, the Eighth Army was facing the Italian-German Panzer Army near the Mareth Line and came under command of General Harold Alexander's 18th Army Group for the concluding phase of the war in North Africa, the Tunisia Campaign. After the Anglo-American landings (Operation Torch) in North-West Africa in November 1942, and subsequent battles against Vichy France forces (who then changed sides), the Allies encircled several thousand German and Italian personnel in northern Tunisia and finally forced their surrender in May 1943.

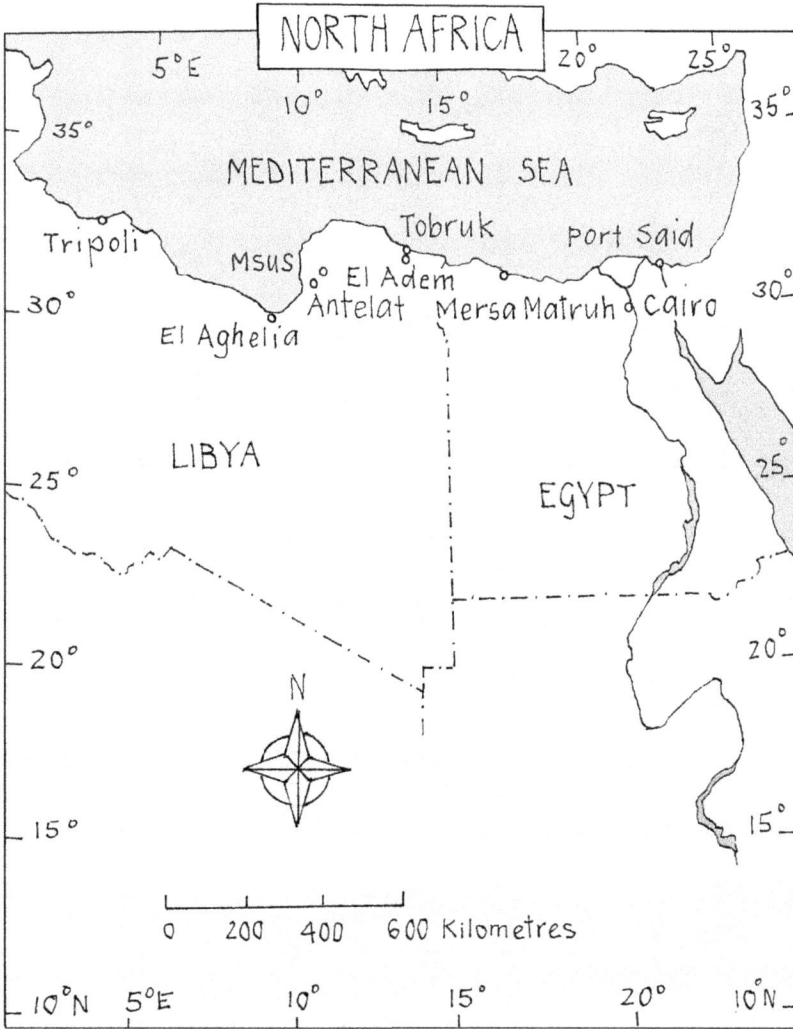

NORTH AFRICA

FIGHTING ROMMEL

Arriving in Egypt in early April 1941 the group travelled by train from Port Said to RAF Station Heliopolis outside Cairo and held in 'pool' positions. While waiting assignment to units the group contributed to the war effort by erecting eight man tents, and rewarded their efforts by building a bar and forming a mess.

Sergeant Jack Bell Cairo 1941

Some pilots were assigned to 3 Squadron and converted to Tomahawks and then Kittyhawks. Not designed for operations in dusty conditions, several pilots were killed after sand entered the engines and seized them unexpectedly. The intake vents were extended further forward through local modifications in order to overcome the problem.

After several weeks of work parties Jack was assigned to No. 216 Squadron RAF in June 1941. The Squadron flew Bristol Bombays, a medium sized transport aircraft, and moved stores, spare parts,

NO. 216 SQUADRON RAF

No. 216 Squadron was formed at Royal Air Force (RAF) Manston by re-numbering No. 16 Squadron Royal Naval Air Service when the RAF was established in 1918. During the Second World War, with a few exceptions, such as the attacks from 17 to 21 June 1940 by single aircraft of No. 216 Squadron on the airfields of El Adem and Tobruk, the unit was principally a transport squadron, operating the Vickers Type 264 Valentia, Bristol Bombay, Vickers Wellington, Lockheed Hudson and Douglas Dakota.

The 216 Squadron Crest

BRISTOL BOMBAY

The Bristol Bombay was a British troop transport aircraft adaptable for use as a medium bomber flown by the Royal Air Force (RAF) during the Second World War. The first production Bombay flew on March 1939, with deliveries to No. 216 Squadron RAF based in Egypt beginning in September that year.

General characteristics:

- Crew: three-four
- Capacity: 24 armed troops or 10 stretchers
- Length: 69 ft 3 in (21.1 m)
- Wingspan: 95 ft 9 in (29.2 m)
- Height: 19 ft 11 in (6.1 m)
- Wing area: 1,340 ft² (124.5 m²)
- Empty weight: 13,800 lb (6,260 kg)
- Loaded weight: 20,180 lb (9,173 kg)
- Power plant: 2 × Bristol Pegasus XXII radial engines, 1,010 hp (755 kW) each

Performance:

- Maximum speed: 167 kn (192 mph, 309 km/h) at 6,500 ft (2,000 m)
- Cruise speed: 139 kn (160 mph, 268 km/h) at 10,000 ft (3,050 m)
- Range: 1,940 nmi (2,230 mi, 3,560 km) with overload fuel
- Service ceiling: 24,850 ft (7,600 m)
- Rate of climb: 750 ft/min (3.8 m/s)
- Wing loading: 14.9 lb/ft² (72.9 kg/m²)
- Power/mass: 0.10 hp/lb (170 W/kg)

Armament:

- Guns: 2 × 0.303 in (7.7 mm) Vickers K machine guns in powered nose and tail turrets
- Bombs: 2,000 lb (907 kg) as 8 × 250 lb (113 kg) bombs on under fuselage racks

Although it was outclassed as a bomber for the European theatre, the Bristol Bombay saw some service with British-based No. 271 Squadron ferrying supplies to the British Expeditionary Force in France in 1940. The Bombay's main service was in the Middle East, particularly with No. 216 Squadron, which operated most of the Bombays built at some stage.

When the war with Italy began in June 1940, in the absence of more modern aircraft, 216 Squadron's Bombays were used as night bombers as well as in their principal role as transport aircraft. The design bombload of 250 lb bombs under the fuselage was supplemented by improvised bombs thrown out of the cargo door by hand. The aircraft flew bombing sorties against targets in the Western Desert, including Benghazi and Tobruk, and against Italian Somaliland, until the build-up of Vickers Wellington bombers in Egypt allowed the Bombays to concentrate on transport operations.

In the transport role, the Bristol Bombay ferried supplies and evacuated the wounded throughout the North African campaign. The multi-purpose interior looked like a tramcar of the period and could be converted in minutes to carry stretchers suspended in two tiers along the fuselage as soon as the outward cargo had been unloaded. Techniques for in-flight casualty care were developed to incorporate blood transfusion facilities and drips. In four years, thousands of Eight Army casualties were evacuated from battle areas by Bristol Bombays.

Bristol Bombay crews spent much of their lives on detachment. Frequently a lone aircraft, or two or three, would be detached 'up the blue' (as distant reaches of the desert were called) for some days at a time. The aircraft then became a flying caravan, the crew living, sleeping, eating on board, organising their own life support provisioning. Sometimes a day or two task would become a week or two task. A 14 gallon water tank was mounted behind the mid-ships bulkhead and topped up at every opportunity. The crews became adept at self-sufficiency, equipping and supplying themselves for the nomadic lifestyle, which getting on with whatever operational task they had been sent out to do.

On 2 May 1941, Bombays of No. 216 Squadron RAF evacuated the Greek Royal Family from Crete to Egypt. Later that month, Bombays played an important role in ferrying troops during the Anglo-Iraqi War. Five Bombays were used by the fledgling Special Air Service in their first official operation in the Middle East, a raid on five forward German aerodromes on 17 November 1941.

The Bristol Bombay

medical supplies and personnel all over Egypt, Libya and Somaliland. The Squadron also flew sorties to Lyddia Airport in Tel Aviv, to Cyprus and return. Jack slowly became aware of the 'on the side' transporting that the crews had taken up as an aside during their missions. Trading their service issued cigarettes for oranges in Tel Aviv, these would then be transported to Cyprus and sold or traded for scotch whiskey, which was then brought back to Heliopolis and sold at the officers' and NCO's messes. When sufficient funds had accumulated a 'free night' would be put on. On these occasions, dress uniforms would be donned, wives and nurses would be invited and the joyous mood would usually continue until the duty officer intervened.

Jack setting up yet one more bloody tent

The Squadron also resupplied units from the Long Range Desert Group with fuel, food and ammunition. The landing sites were an area of natural ground often between low-lying hills so as to provide cover from observation. Difficult to locate due to the lack of markers in the terrain, once landed the cargo would have to be unloaded hastily in the event of detection and attack. Typically, the Long Range Desert Group would only come out of hiding to retrieve the stores as the aircraft was leaving. Another task was to help train the Special Air Service soldiers to parachute—sometimes from as low as 500 feet.

On 1 September 1941 Jack was promoted to Flight Sergeant.

On the night of 16 November 1941 General Claude Auchinleck and the allies launched Operation Crusader. Three aircraft from 216 Squadron were tasked to parachute Special Air Service teams behind enemy lines. One aircraft never returned and is believed to have crashed without any survivors. Strong winds caused the aircraft and the parachutists to be dropped well away from their designated landing zones. Some bands managed to form and did as much damage to the Germans as they could. One group infiltrated an airfield and destroyed a number of fighter aircraft with plastic explosives placed on the wings.

LONG RANGE DESERT GROUP

The Long Range Desert Group (LRDG) was a reconnaissance and raiding unit of the British Army during the Second World War.

Originally called the Long Range Patrol (LRP), the unit was founded in Egypt in June 1940 by Major Ralph A. Bagnold, acting under the direction of General Archibald Wavell. Bagnold was assisted by Captain Patrick Clayton and Captain William Shaw. At first the majority of the men were from New Zealand, but they were soon joined by Southern Rhodesian and British volunteers, whereupon new sub-units were formed and the name was changed to the better-known Long Range Desert Group (LRDG). The LRDG never numbered more than 350 men, all of whom were volunteers.

The LRDG was formed specifically to carry out deep penetration, covert reconnaissance patrols and intelligence missions from behind Italian lines, although they sometimes engaged in combat operations. Because the LRDG were experts in desert navigation they were sometimes assigned to guide other units, including the Special Air Service and secret agents across the desert. During the Desert Campaign between December 1940 and April 1943, the vehicles of the LRDG operated constantly behind the Axis lines, missing a total of only 15 days during the entire period. Possibly their most notable offensive action was during Operation Caravan, an attack on the town of Barce and its associated airfield, on the night of 13 September 1942. However, their most vital role was the 'Road Watch', during which they clandestinely monitored traffic on the main road from Tripoli to Benghazi, transmitting the intelligence to British Army Headquarters.

With the surrender of the Axis forces in Tunisia in May 1943, the LRDG changed roles and moved operations to the eastern Mediterranean, carrying out missions in the Greek islands, Italy and the Balkans. After the end of the war in Europe, the leaders of the LRDG made a request to the War Office for the unit to be transferred to the Far East to conduct operations against the Japanese Empire. The request was declined and the LRDG was disbanded in August 1945.

SPECIAL AIR SERVICE

The Special Air Service (SAS) was a unit of the British Army during the Second World War that was formed in July 1941 by David Stirling and originally called 'L' Detachment, Special Air Service Brigade—the 'L' designation and Air Service name being a tie-in to a British disinformation campaign, trying to deceive the Axis into thinking there was a paratrooper regiment with numerous units operating in the area (the real SAS would 'prove' to the Axis that the fake one existed).

It was conceived as a commando force to operate behind enemy lines in the North African Campaign and initially consisted of five officers and 60 other ranks. Its first mission, in November 1941, was a parachute drop in support of the Operation Crusader offensive. Due to German resistance and adverse weather conditions, the mission was a disaster; 22 men, a third of the unit, were killed or captured. The SAS's second mission was a major success. Transported by the Long Range Desert Group, it attacked three airfields in Libya, destroying 60 aircraft with the loss of two men and three Jeeps. In September 1942, it was renamed 1st SAS, consisting at that time of four British squadrons, one Free French, one Greek, and the Folboat Section.

Passengers bound for various locations in the Western Desert, sitting in a Bristol Bombay of No. 216 Squadron RAF based at Heliopolis, Egypt

RAF officers haul their luggage from a Bristol Bombay of No. 216 Squadron RAF after landing at Maleme, Crete

A Long Range Desert Group Patrol

Another task for the Squadron during Operation Crusader was to land short of the battle area and evacuate wounded soldiers—either to the field hospital or back to Alexandria or Cairo. Jack observed that tank crews were underrepresented amongst the wounded as they were often killed rather than wounded because of the enemy '88's' armour piercing rounds were fired with deadly effect from well outside of the tank's gun range. In order to keep up with the Allied advance the Squadron jumped forward to an air base near Mersa Matruh.

A British Crusader tank passed a burning Panzer IV tank during Operation Crusader

As Rommel's forces were forced back the besieged garrison at Tobruk was relieved on 27 November 1941. 216 Squadron was moved forward again to El Adem—on the escarpment south of Tobruk. From here Jack had the opportunity to visit Tobruk and witness first-hand the destruction those months of fighting over this strategically important port had caused.

Only a few hours after a group from the Long Range Desert Group captured the Quetta Fort in southern Libya, John's aircraft flew in to resupply them. He heard that in order to drive out occupying Italians they had circled the fort with their vehicles firing their .5 inch machine guns while their only heavy weapon, a Bofors gun, fired a couple of rounds and then moved to an new position. Eventually the Italian captain in command of the fort surrendered explaining later that he feared for the safety of the women in the fort. The allies had to accept a large number of prisoners and Jack's aircraft evacuated wounded Allied and Italian soldiers. Twenty years later Jack would coincidentally meet this Italian captain again, who after seeing out the rest of the war as a prisoner returned to his family business running a silk mill in Como, Italy.

An Indian soldier guards a group of Italian prisoners near El Adem aerodrome, during the pursuit of Axis forces westwards after the relief of Tobruk

While at El Adem Jack and his observer crew mate—Tony Carter—decided that they needed a 'decent' vehicle to get around in. Allied vehicles being in short supply, the pair visited the captured vehicles compound and for two pounds purchased an Auto Union (the forerunner to Audi) 'escape' wagon. The area around the driver and passenger seats had been fitted with steel plates to protect the occupants. With a double ratio gearbox, five forward and three reverse gears it was highly mobile in the soft sand and had a (verified) top speed of 185 km/hr. Sadly, the four Spandau .5 inch machine guns mounted on two posts either side of the vehicle had been removed. The car was later used as the airport duty officers' vehicle.

One night during a sandstorm Jack and his mates heard a Wellington bomber above the air field searching for the landing ground. After a while the motors cut down and the morning revealed that the aircraft had come down at the edge of the airfield. Covered in sand and unable to be recovered it was stripped over the next few days for spare parts.

While picking up some personnel at Landing Ground 130 Jack's aircraft was suddenly set upon by two Messerschmitt Bf 109 fighters. While the Bombay Bristol sat vulnerably at the base of a sand hill the crew sought

A pair of Messerschmitt Bf 109 fighters over North Africa

Wrecked Italian aircraft at El Adem airfield, Libya

cover by running over the top of the sand hill opposite to the direction of the attacking planes. The Messerschmitt's made two passes before heading off. Miraculously, they had put dozens of rounds through the Bombay but it hadn't started burning and all the crew were uninjured. Jack's crew managed to get the Bombay airborne and retuned to base. On landing they blew a tyre and the aircraft skewed and the frame was twisted out of shape.

Not long after this close call Jack was returned to Cairo for a week suffering from suspected dengue fever. When he returned to El Adem Jack was offered the chance to apply for a commission but declined.

Despite achieving a number of tactical successes, Rommel was forced to concede Tobruk and was pushed back to El Agheila by the end of 1941. The battle paused and Rommel had the opportunity to re-group and re-supply.

On 26 November 1941 the Commander-in-Chief Middle East Command, General Sir Claude Auchinleck, replaced the Commander of the Eighth Army, Lieutenant General Alan Cunningham with Major General Neil Ritchie, following disagreements between Auchinleck and Cunningham.

A few weeks later on 21 January 1942 Rommel launched a counter-attack with an armoured 'reconnaissance in force'. Finding the Eighth Army forward elements dispersed and tired, in his typical manner, he took advantage of the situation. By 23 January 1942 the Axis forces had advanced to recapture Ajedabia and the front line continued to be pushed back East.

BUMPING INTO THE
15TH PANZER DIVISION

On 23 January 1942 two aircraft—a Bristol Bombay and a De Havilland DH86 Ambulance—were dispatched early in the morning to collect some members of Lieutenant General Cunningham's staff and exchange aircrew at Msus.

Sergeant Jack Bell was assigned to Bristol Bombay Number L5811 with Flying Officer F. Wilcox, RAF as the first pilot, 88435 Flying Officer James N.E. Bateman, RAF as the second pilot and Australian 402012 Sergeant Anthony Edward Carter—Jack's partner in crime with the escape wagon—as the navigator. In the back of the aircraft a fitter and a rigger completed the aircrew and a number of other replacement aircrew were travelling as passengers.

The flight path was to take them south west over Magtuaed Saud—an oasis and way marker—and then north east to Msus. There was a heavy mist and navigation proved challenging so the pilot flew low to try and identify landmarks. Sensing that they were off course and probably south of Msus the pilot turned north when the aircraft 'bumped' into the rapidly advancing 15th Panzer Division.

A large high explosive shell fired from the ground hit the aircraft behind the cockpit and exploded. To this day, no one is quite sure what type of gun fired the shell but in all probability it was from an 88 mm cannon.

An 88 mm cannon firing

15TH PANZER DIVISION

The 15th Panzer Division was an armoured division in the German Army, the Wehrmacht, during the Second World War, established in 1940. The division, formed from the 33rd Infantry Division, fought exclusively in North Africa from 1941 to 1943, eventually ceasing to exist after surrendering in Tunisia in May 1943.

The 33rd Infantry Division, forerunner of the 15th Panzer Division, was formed in April 1936 and part of the German defences in the Saarland during the early month of the war. It participated in the invasion of France and remained there after the French surrender as an occupation force. It returned to Germany in September 1940 to be converted to a tank division.

The division was transported to Libya in April 1941, joining General Erwin Rommel's Deutsches Afrikakorps (DAK) as one of two German tank divisions in North Africa at the time, the other having been the 21st Panzer Division. The division took part in all major

German operations in North Africa except the first, for which it arrived too late. It was part of the successful German defence against British attempts to relieve Tobruk, Operation Brevity and Operation Battleaxe. On 18 November 1941 British forces began Operation Crusader with the objective of relieving the besieged forces at Tobruk. The 15th Panzer Division was situated to the east of Tobruk, suffered severe losses and was forced to retreat west.

The 15th Panzer Division was part of the German offensive in January 1942 that retook Benghazi. It participated in the battle of Gazala, the capture of Tobruk and the German invasion of Egypt which came to a stand-still at El Alamein. The division suffered severe loses at the second battle of El Alamein in November 1942 and was forced to retreat along with the rest of the Afrikakorps.

After the retreat of the Axis forces to Tunisia the 15th Panzer Division was part of the battle of Kasserine Pass against inexperienced United States forces in February 1943. The division eventually surrendered alongside other Axis forces in Tunisia in May 1943 and was not re-established.

Panzer III of the 15th Panzer Division in Column

8.8 CM FLAK 18/36/37/41

The 8.8 cm Flak (commonly called the eighty-eight) was a German 88 mm anti-aircraft and anti-tank artillery gun during the Second World War. It was widely used by Germany throughout the war, and was one of the most recognized German weapons of that conflict. Development of the original model led to a wide variety of guns. The name applies to a series of related guns, the first one officially called the 8.8 cm Flak 18, the improved 8.8 cm Flak 36, and later the 8.8 cm Flak 37. Flak is a contraction of German Flugzeugabwehrkanone meaning 'aircraft-defence cannon', the original purpose of the eighty-eight. In English, 'flak' became a generic term for ground anti-aircraft fire. In informal German use, the guns were universally known as the Acht-acht (eight-eight).

The 8.8cm Flak in action

The versatile carriage allowed the eighty-eight to be fired in a limited anti-tank mode when still on its wheels; it could be completely emplaced in only two-and-a-half minutes. Its successful use as an improvised anti-tank

gun led to the development of a tank gun based upon it:
the 8.8 cm KwK 36, with the 'KwK' abbreviation standing
for Kampfwagen-Kanone (literally battle vehicle cannon,
or main battle tank cannon), meant to be placed in a gun
turret as the tank's primary armament. This gun served
as the main armament of the Tiger I heavy tank.

Twenty-five year old Sergeant Anthony Carter was killed immediately. Shrapnel ripped through the plane. Flying Officer Wilcox, the first pilot, was severely wounded in the right leg. Flying Officer Bateman received a number of small shrapnel wounds. Jack Bell—sitting only a metre away from Tony Carter but shielded to some degree by the wireless set—was wounded with a large piece of shrapnel in his abdomen, and smaller pieces lodged in his right leg and right arm.

With no parachutes and the plane on fire and losing altitude quickly the crew had little choice but to try and land the aircraft. Flying Officer Bateman managed to get the damaged plane on the ground but in the landing Jack bumped a radio set and received a nasty cut to his head. Bateman then opened the hatch forward of the navigators station and directed Jack to go out the aft exit and come around to help lift Wilcox out.

As Jack went out the rear exit he called out for the other crew members and passengers—some wounded with shrapnel and burns—to help but they either didn't hear him or chose to ignore him as they distanced themselves from the burning aircraft. Jack went back to the front of the plane and with Bateman managed to get Wilcox out of the cockpit before dragging him about 50 yards away. Through the process the side of Jack's head and hands were badly burned—particularly his right hand.

While the aircraft was being evacuated the DH86 Ambulance that was travelling with them landed alongside to see if they could rescue the survivors. The pilot of the DH86 assumed that the Bristol Bombay had been shot down by 'friendly fire', but he soon realised that this wasn't the case as the Germans quickly approached both aircraft.

By this stage Jack was lying in the gritty sand about 30 metres away from a burning aircraft and starting to drift out and in of consciousness.

A De Havilland DH86 Ambulance in flight

The Bristol Bombay Bomber-Transport

(Two 1,010 h.p. Bristol Pegasus XXII motors).

Built by Short and Harland Ltd. in Belfast.

Jack's seat

Cut-Away of the Bristol Bombay showing Jack's Seat

44

ITALY, AUSTRIA and GERMANY

In the Bag in Italy

They were all quickly rounded up by the Germans and were now Prisoners of War. The injured were placed in an ambulance and taken to a field hospital just outside of Antelat. Despite Red Cross markings on the Ambulance Allied fighters strafed the vehicle during the trip.

Flying Officer Wilcox's right leg was so badly damaged that the doctors at the field hospital had no option other than to remove it. It is believed that he was later repatriated back to the UK.

Jack was operated on to have a large splinter of metal removed from his abdomen. As a consequence of the operation he had to have a 'few inches' of his small intestine removed. The smaller pieces of shrapnel in his arms and legs were not removed with the hope that they might 'work their way out' over time; they never did and remain there to this day. Jack's right hand was so badly burned that it began to curl inwards and the fingers became locked in a 'cupped' position. After a few days the doctors cut away the dead brown skin from his palm and slowly he managed to be able to move his fingers again.

The staff at No. 216 Squadron soon learned that the Bristol Bombay had been shot down and that some of the crew and passengers had been taken captive—but they didn't know who might have been killed or injured. The RAAF could do little else but report that Jack was missing in action. Within a few days this advice had been relayed by telegram to his mother and father. So began a period of anxiety where his next of kin didn't know whether Jack was dead or alive.

In the days after the operation Jack got to know the German surgeon that had operated on him. As luck would have it he was an abdominal specialist who had trained and practiced in England. The surgeon's English was very good and Jack learned that he had moved to the UK after the First World War. He consulted from rooms in the prestigious Harley Street in Marylebone, London and occasional undertook work in Germany. On one of these trips in 1939 the doctor was refused permission to return to England. He was subsequently drafted to work for the Army but explained to Jack that because of his English connections was not fully trusted by his workmates.

With the German advance the field hospital was required to move east and so Jack and one other badly injured prisoner were transferred over to the Italians. If they had been 'walking wounded' they would have been put into the German POW system and moved to Germany.

Ten days after his surgery Jack was transported on a stretcher in the back of a 3 ton truck to a hospital in Tripoli. The 650 km trip along the bumpy coast road took four days. The canvas covering the back of the truck provided little relief from the blistering heat. Each night they were taken off the truck to sleep and Jack recalls that Italian orderlies looking after them were 'not very gentle'. Jack's only saving grace was that his German surgeon had given him ten vials of morphine for the trip; which Jack injected each morning and night. By the time he reached Tripoli Jack's stomach wound had completely opened up.

In the hospital in Tripoli Jack was put in his own room and received his first proper meal in about two weeks—a small bowl of pasta served to him by an Italian nun. She cried as she fed him. Sadly, within an hour Jack had brought it all back up again, so she then brought him a bowl of stewed quince. She also gave Jack a sponge bath and removed all the oil, dirt and blood that had built up on him over the preceding days. While Jack was not fully aware of his surroundings he would long remember the compassion this woman showed towards him. But not all the hospital staff were as compassionate; not long after he was admitted to this hospital Jack's shoes, socks and trousers were stolen while he was asleep.

In hospital Jack was registered as a POW with the International Committee for the Red Cross. This humanitarian organisation registered all POWs and provided prisoner lists of names and locations to all sides of the conflict. This is most often how a person went from being listed as 'missing in action' to POW—a huge relief to family and friends. By 16 February 1942 the RAAF was able to officially list Jack as a POW and provided formal advice via a registered letter to his family on 23 March 1942—although without any details about his injuries. At this stage Jack's mother had moved into the holiday house at Sandgate and Jack's father had joined his older brother Laurie working on a pineapple farm up in the Glasshouse Mountains. Ironically, the farm employed Italian POWs who had been captured in Abyssinia (present day Ethiopia).

INTERNATIONAL COMMITTEE FOR THE RED CROSS

The Geneva Convention of 27 July 1929 Relative to the Treatment of Prisoners of War (POW) gave captives a certain number of rights which they could claim from the authorities detaining them. In addition, under this Convention the International Committee for the Red Cross (ICRC) was entitled to enquire about what had become of POWs and to make proposals regarding improvements in their detention conditions.

As in the First World War, one of the ICRC's first steps after hostilities broke out in 1939 was to establish a clearing house for information on POWs. On the basis of the Convention the ICRC opened The Central Agency for Prisoners of War, which performed three tasks:

- centralising all information on POWs (notices of capture, transfer, death, etc.);
- handing over this information to the POWs' countries of origin;
- keeping up contact between the POWs and their families (passing on family messages).

During the Second World War, the Central Agency for POWs occupied a large building in Geneva. As the conflict wore on, additional offices were set up in other buildings, mainly hotels. Altogether, 27 branch offices were opened.

The blinding speed of the major military offensives led to the capture of huge numbers of POWs: over 600,000 Poles in September 1939; almost two million men (Dutch, Belgian, English and French) during the 1940 campaign; some five million Soviets on the Eastern front from the summer of 1941 onwards. Then, in May 1945, Germany's entire army fell into the hands of the Allies after the country's surrender, and finally, in September 1945, the whole Japanese army was taken into captivity. These prisoners of war were scattered throughout the world. The main camps, which were inhabited by tens of thousands of prisoners, were the size of towns.

In order to obtain as much information as possible on prisoners of war, the ICRC relied mainly on lists sent to it by the warring countries that had captured the prisoners, but it supplemented this information with enquiries conducted in the camps by its delegates. From the time hostilities began, ICRC delegates visited prisoners of war. The first visits were made between

23 and 26 September 1939, when an ICRC delegate entered three camps for Polish POWs in Germany.

Throughout the war, ICRC delegates continued systematically to visit prisoner-of-war camps: their main concern was to monitor what was happening to the captives and to improve their conditions of detention. The delegates soon realized that the Axis powers were in no position to provide for the upkeep of the millions of Allied POWs who had fallen into their hands. The shortages that prevailed throughout Europe made it impossible to obtain the supplies needed for them. The ICRC therefore entered into negotiations to get authorization to procure goods for this purpose outside Europe.

On 29 August 1940, the British government agreed that collective relief could be sent to POWs, on condition that the way this relief was being used would be subject to strict monitoring designed to guarantee that it was not going to help the Axis war effort. Thus, each relief consignment sent had to receive special authorization, each time requiring new negotiations on the part of the ICRC.

Owing to the dismantling of all transport networks, the ICRC had to set up a vast logistical operation for dispatching the relief supplies: chartering ships on the open sea under its own emblem; setting up huge warehouses at each stage, in Lisbon, Marseille, Göteborg, Lübeck, Geneva, and so on. From Switzerland, the supplies were sent on to Germany in sealed railway wagons. After the German railway network was destroyed, the goods travelled in convoys of trucks. A combination of strict bookkeeping of the receipts signed by persons trusted by the prisoners of war, together with spot checks carried out by ICRC delegates during their visits, made it possible to ensure that the relief was not diverted.

Thanks to the supplies sent to the ICRC by the countries of origin of the POW, each according to its means, the organization managed to provide four standard five-kg parcels per month to each American and British prisoner, and one or two parcels per month to prisoners of other nationalities. This meant monthly trips made by around 2,000 railway wagons, involving a total of 430,000 tonnes of supplies, or 90 million individual parcels. These supplies improved the living conditions of millions of prisoners of war.

During the war, the ICRC also negotiated the repatriation of disabled prisoners. It succeeded in bringing 35,000 people back home - half of these were war wounded, while the others were medical personnel and civilians. The ICRC also visited German POWs of war in the hands of the Allies, except in the USSR.

In April 1945, the ICRC had a total staff of 3,921, 2,585 of whom were working for the Agency. The ICRC registered POWs and communicated essential information about them to their families by using 'capture cards' and 'individual id entity cards'. The Agency also undertook to forward prisoners' correspondence. In total, over six years, the Agency filled in around 25 million of these 'individual identity cards' and passed on some 120 million messages, carrying news to and from POWs and their families.

After a week in Tripoli Jack was put onto a hospital ship bound for Caserta Hospital on the outskirts of Naples. The ship had uninjured POWs as well as walking wounded and seriously injured. Medical staff were few and so the uninjured POWs cared for those that needed assistance. Jack, for example, was unable to go to the toilet without a significant amount of assistance from others. The senior nurse on the ship was Countess Ciano—Il Duce's daughter. Jack recalls that she was 'a fine looking woman' and spent a lot of time talking to all the Italian and Allied wounded. On 16 February 1942, whilst at sea,

Countess Ciano (Edda Mussolini)

the news came that Singapore had fallen to the Japanese; disbelief eventually turned into deep concern about the consequences. The prospect of this being a long war—and one that might not be won by the Allies—loomed large in the minds of the prisoners.

Taken into the Caserta Hospital Jack spent several weeks recovering from his injuries and surgery. Food was scarce and fresh fruit non-existent, however, the hospital backed onto the grounds of Prince Umberto's Summer Palace which contained hundreds of fruit trees. Jack recalls looking out of his window at the ripe fruit dropping onto the ground and rotting.

While in Caserta Hospital Jack was also exposed to the divide between white and black soldiers from South Africa. Two black soldiers felt so intimidated by two white soldiers that they refrained from applying to be repatriated. Others made their case on their behalf and one of the two black soldiers was selected to be sent home.

By early March 1942 Jack had recovered sufficiently to be transferred to the Parma Hospital in the north of Italy. He had lost a lot of weight and was down to 6 stone 4 pounds—or about 40 kg. The atmosphere at Parma was much more positive and eventually Jack began to walk again—albeit bent over like an old man. Over time his health and posture both improved. Jack's movements and condition were being monitored by the Red Cross and reports about his location and the state of his injuries were regularly relayed back to Australia and then to his next of kin.

As prisoner's health improved, however, so did their desire to escape and 'Skipper' Palmer, a lieutenant commander in the Royal Australian Navy, tried to make a break at the end of May. He was caught and brought back to the hospital. While Skipper was being questioned one of the Italian guards recognised a block of chocolate that he had traded with Jack in return for his watch. Jack was accused of organising the escape and after being berated transferred out of the hospital to Campo 65—a 'proper' POW camp—at Gravina-Altamura in the south of Italy. Knowing that his life was about to get a bit tougher Jack's RAAF mate Bob Malloch gave him a few bits and pieces to help along the road. Given Jack's evidently dangerous nature he was escorted by a Sergeant and three privates for the overnight train journey and civilians were kept out of the carriage. At the station Jack flashed the 'V' for Victory sign and some of the locals got agitated and spat on him.

Campo 65 was the main transit camp for all new POWs. In June it was very hot during the day and very cold at night. The conditions and food were 'appalling'. Jack took his turn as the rations Sergeant and took delivery of a 48 hour weekend ration break for 700 men: 14 cabbages, 11 cauliflowers and four bunches of fennel. One serve of thin soup on each day was all that these rations allowed. Water was only made available to the prisoners for one hour a day so containers had to be filled to allow drinking outside of this hour. Jack recalls that the conditions were so terrible that about 5 to 6 prisoners died each week.

CAMPO 65 GRAVINA-ALTAMURA

Campo 65 was a Prisoner of War (POW) camp situated close to the city of Gravina-Altamura in central Southern Italy. Campo 65 was established in early 1942 as a transit camp for Allied non-commissioned ranks captured in North Africa. When Allied troops invaded Sicily during July/August 1943 the camp was cleared and internees were moved to other camps including Campo 57.

Allied POWs cooking in the basic conditions at Campo 65

Sergeant Major Alan Beecroft

Jack was only held at Campo 65 for four weeks before being transferred in early July 1942 to Campo 57 at Grupignano in the north east of Italy. Campo 57 was designated for 'Dominion forces' but was largely filled with Australian and New Zealand POWs. Jack was assigned to Number 2 compound commanded by an Australian Army Warrant Officer—Alan Beecroft from Tasmania.

Compared to Campo 65, Campo 57 was well established and well regulated. The engineer POWs had constructed latrines and showers and strict health regulations were imposed including showers and foot inspections. Enlisted POWs were sent out to work on local farms and in return received additional rations. The Italians didn't issue POW numbers but the camp used a system of hut and bunk numbers to assign everyone a number. These were used at meal times where everyone lined up in number order to receive their ration.

The food consisted of the Italian army ration of bread, macaroni or rice, and other staple items. The Italian ration scales (grams daily) for POWs was supposed to be:

CAMPO 57 GRUPIGNANO

Campo 57 was a Prisoner of War camp situated close to the village of Grupignano near Udine in Northern Italy. The camp principally held Australian and New Zealand non-commissioned soldiers with smaller numbers of British, Indian and South African men during Second World War.

Prisoners were transported to Campo 57 by train with the last leg of transportation terminating at Cividale. The POWs were then marched through the hamlet of Premariacco to the site of the camp. The camp itself was set on flat terrain proximal to the river Natsionne. Surrounding the camp was predominantly farming land.

On the chosen site for Campo 57 was a chapel known as San Mauro. The chapel was torn down to allow construction of the camp but was rebuilt by prisoners of war in 1943. The chapel still stands today and inside bears the signature of the POWs that rebuilt it.

Campo 57 held some 20 officers and 4,570 other ranks. The prison buildings consisted of two compounds, each with its own cook-house, ablution block, recreation huts and orderly rooms. The dormitory huts were made of double wooden walls located on concrete foundations, with a melthoid (felt impregnated with bitumen) roof, and one heating stove for which there never appeared to be any fuel. Sleeping accommodation was in wooden double bunks in groups of eight. Each hut held approximately 50 prisoners, and each compound had 20 huts, the Hut Commander slept in an area which doubled as an administration office. From the Camp looking north through the perimeter barbed wire system, there was a spectacular view of the Dolomites and the mountains of nearby Yugoslavia. The scenery was magnificent, even when viewed through barbed wire spectacles.

By June 1942, Campo 57 held some 2,000 Australian and New Zealand POWs. As the fierce fighting around El Alamein saw many Allied POWs taken by Rommel's forces, but handed over to the Italians, the Italian authorities pushed forward their expansion plans, and two new compounds, 3 and 4, arose to extend the already operative compounds 1 and 2. By the end of 1942, the four compounds were home to some 4,000 Australian and New Zealand POWs.

The main entrance to Campo 57 in northern Italy
with Carabinieri guards on sentry duty

Looking along the main road of Campo 57
from the main entrance

The POW huts behind the inner fence of barbed wire at Campo 57

The POW huts behind the inner fence of barbed wire at Campo 57.
Note the barbed wire entanglement in the foreground

The POW huts are behind an inner fence of barbed wire at Campo
57. There are two fences with barbed wire entanglement between
and stones mark the zone in between the trip wire and inner fence.
This area is strictly out of bounds and prisoners would be shot if
caught there. Guard watch towers are placed around this perimeter.
In the background is the partially erected Roman Catholic Chapel
which the POWs are working on with Italian stonemasons

The Kitchen block at Campo 57. Photographed by Lee Hill in 1943

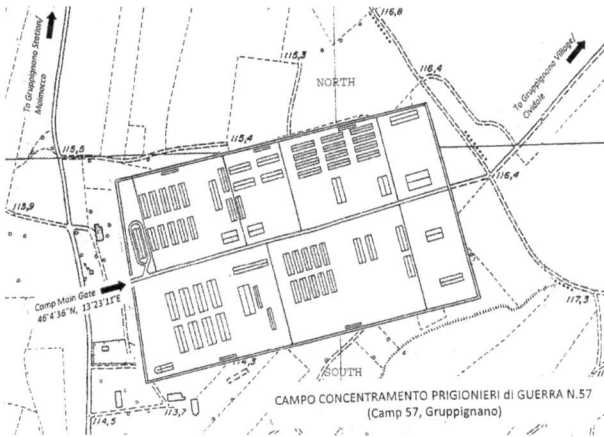

CAMPO CONCENTRAMENTO PRIGIONIERI di GUERRA N.57
(Camp 57, Gruppignano)

The layout of Campo 57

Meal time at Campo 57

	Officers	Other Ranks (non-working)	Other Ranks (working)
Bread	150	200	400
Macaroni or rice	66	66	120
Fat	10	13	13
Sugar	16	15	15
Cheese (cooking)	10	10	10
Cheese (table)	When available	30	43
Meat	14	34	34
Tomato puree	15	15	15
Egg	1 a month	1 a month	1 a month
Peas and beans	15	30	30
Coffee substitute	7	7	7

The estimated calorific values for the three columns above are 780, 1,081 and 1,821. The modern recommended daily calorific intake for an active young man is 3,000 calories per day. Red Cross parcels were welcome supplements and enabled a vibrant bartering trade in items between the POWs and their guards; for example, a tin of coffee could be exchanged for one or two loaves of bread as coffee was in great demand by the Italians, even though they were as hungry as the POWs. POWs also received clothing parcels from home.

The POWs would periodically receive a few lira of 'camp money' printed on heavy card. Those with camp money could buy cigarettes, toiletries, packs of cards, Italian newspapers and even wine from the camp shop. Officers were sometimes able to buy green vegetables, small amounts of salted fish, fresh and dried fruit, wine and cakes; other ranks only occasionally.

Exercise and sport were all part of the daily routine—at least when the weather allowed. POWs spent a lot of time reading paperbacks sent

RED CROSS PARCELS

Red Cross parcels are packages containing mostly food, tobacco and personal hygiene items sent by the International Association of the Red Cross to prisoners of war during the First and Second World Wars. The Red Cross arranged them in accordance with the provisions of the Geneva Convention of 1929. During World War II these packages augmented the often-meagre and deficient diets in the POW camps, contributing greatly to prisoner survival and an increase in morale.

Australian Red Cross Society workers packing food parcels for Australians held in POW camps

Typical contents of a Red Cross Parcel

Unidentified POWs at Campo 57.
Photograph taken by Lee Hill circa 1941

POWs lined up for a kit inspection at Campo 57.
Photograph taken by Lee Hill in December 1941

Roman Catholic Service at Campo 57

The New Zealand and Australian POWs in Campo 57 who formed the camp's
news staff enjoying a beer at the entrance to the camp canteen.
From left to right: Private Andrews, AIF, Private Lee Hill, 2nd New Zealand
Expeditionary Force, Sergeant Richard Head, AIF and an unidentified Sergeant.
Photograph taken by Lee Hill in 1943

POWs preparing to depart Campo 57 for Germany
September 1943

from home and these were shared around the camp. Playing chess and bridge were also popular pastimes. Groups held classes, put on floor shows and every now and again a game of two-up would 'just happen'.

Jack tried to multiply his camp money by being a 'tail' better in the two-up games. He figured that odds were greater but the rewards better. One game had 13 straight pairs of tails and Jack ended up with a small 'fortune' in camp money. He organised a bunch of his mates to 'blitz' the camp shop with the aim of buying all the available beer. Having achieved that Jack and his mate Butch started a big drinking session and managed to essentially wipe out 24 hours of the war.

Mail was the most precious commodity and any deliveries were warmly received. Invariably letters and packages were held in post offices along the journey and weeks would pass without any mail and then a large delivery would arrive.

Governance over the POW camps in Italy was by a special corps known as the Carabinieri who had both military and civil powers

An Italian card that allowed POWs to advise family of their location

and acted as a type of military police. The Camp was controlled by Lieutenant Colonel Vittorio Calcaterra who prided himself on his strict discipline, and who boasted that his prison was 'escape-proof'. Calcaterra was enemy number one to the POWs. He inspired his men to harsh treatment of the POWs by limiting rations, regular and unwarranted incarnation in the 'boob', and cruel punishments. He was succinctly summed up by A.V.W 'Bluey' Rymer, an Australian wireless operator/airgunner, as 'a short-arsed, fat-gutted little shit. If you were sitting on one side of the camp and you did not get up and stand to attention, it was into the 'boob' with bread and water'. Thanks to Colonel Calcaterra, conditions in Campo 57 were harsh. Food was poor, and housing was crowded and insanitary. The prisoners had to improvise their own medical treatment, coping with the '57 twins', pneumonia and kidney disease. Calcaterra's regime reduced the camp to 'a mass of neurosis as no one knew when his turn would come' to be victimised.

Jack's mate Butch was responsible for taking food to the 'boob' where POWs were placed in confinement. At that time the boob was located at the end of Jack and Butch's hut. Each night some boards were removed that allowed the confinees to slip out and go back to their huts for a feed or some supplies. A brick confinement block was then built outside the camp. Butch was still responsible for delivering the rations and carried them in a bucket. A false bottom was installed in the bucket and contraband smuggled into the new boob. Luckily, Butch was never caught.

On 13 October 1942 nineteen Australian and New Zealand POWs did escape from Campo 57. They began a tunnel under the floor of a disused hut, using only a steel helmet and a small pick. They dug down 16 feet and then excavated a horizontal shaft around 50 yards under the wire apron and into the maize field beyond. On the chosen night 19 men crawled through the tunnel and emerged in the moonlit field. It soon began to rain and this helped cover their escape. They were:

9623 Warrant Officer Class 2 Leslie Boult—27th Machine Gun Battalion

917 Private Hector A. Brien—5th Field Regiment, New Zealand Artillery

5071 Sergeant Thomas Eric Canning—RAAF

A402111 Sergeant Thomas B. Comins—RAAF

SX1008 Sergeant Richard L. Head—2nd/10th Infantry Battalion

VX38981 Warrant Officer Class 2 Archibald Noble—2nd/24th Infantry Battalion

VX29686 Sergeant Gordon C. 'Pud' Poidevin—2nd/24th Infantry Battalion

VX31146 Private William Sloan—2nd/24th Infantry Battalion

VX15912 Sergeant Albert 'Bill' Williams—2nd/24th Infantry Battalion

WX6351 Lance Corporal John D. Costello—2nd/28th Infantry Battalion

WX7120 Private Stanley Lang—2nd/28th Infantry Battalion

7151 Sergeant John F. O'Brien—20th Battalion

NX3134 Gunner George Cotter—2nd/1st Regiment, Royal Australian Artillery

NX3203 Gunner John A. Dwyer—2nd/1st Regiment, Royal Australian Artillery

NX3374 Lance Bombardier Charles Lind—2nd/1st Regiment, Royal Australian Artillery

33965 Sapper Roy Natusch—6th Field Company

NX29943 Corporal David King—2nd/1st Pioneers

SX2242 Private Kevin O'Connell—2nd/1st Pioneers

QX930 Sapper Robert St. Q. Hooper—2nd/7th Field Company, Royal Australian Engineers

Jack knew the first listed seven of these men well. The alarm was raised at roll call the next morning and it was not long before the men were recaptured. Two of the men were on the run for five days, but they still shared the same fate as the others. Most were stripped naked and beaten by the Italian guards, then thrown into solitary confinement on starvation rations. The camp commandant Colonel Calcaterra gave the rest of the camp a hard time in reprisal, even instructing the guards to puncture the Red Cross food tins so that they could not be hoarded for future escape attempts.

In December 1942 the POWs received a small booklet from the Pope to celebrate Christmas.

The receipt of Red Cross parcels was irregular and in March 1943 the Camp Commandant announced that the Red Cross parcels would be cut back from one between four men to one between six. The POWs believed that the Italians were deliberately trying to keep them weak to discourage escapes or mass break outs. Many POWs also developed Beri Beri from a lack of vitamin B. Jack recalls helping the camp medic— Captain Levins from Adelaide—to cook up Pig Weed and other grasses to try and help them.

Unknown to Jack the RAAF promoted him to Warrant Officer with retrospective effect from 1 May 1943. The idea here was to ensure that Jack was not disadvantaged relative to his peers for being a POW. While he was a POW his pay and leave entitlements continued to accrue. Jack didn't find out about his promotion until he got to London at the end of the war.

In the summer of 1943 Jack was horrified when one of his mates was shot dead by a guard. 'Socks' Simmonds was mucking around well inside the compound and acted the fool near one of the guards. The guard simply raised his rifle and shot Socks dead. The guard must have claimed that Socks was trying to escape so instead of being charged he was rewarded with 1500 lira for stopping a prisoner escaping. The camp leaders made a careful note of the guards' details for later action.

When the Allies landed in Sicily in July 1943 the attitude of the Italians changed dramatically for the better. Treatment became less harsh and rations and Red Cross parcels flowed more freely. The Italians were looking to the future and wanted to be 'friends' with the winning team. As the Allies advanced up the Italian Peninsula the mood amongst the POWs improved as the prospect of liberation grew. But when Italy capitulated on 3 September 1943 the Germans had other ideas and quickly took control of all the POW camps.

My mid-September they learned that the Germans planned to move them to POW camps in Germany. So, after 14 months in Campo 57 the POWs were told to pack all their belongings and were herded into closed train wagons; packed like sardines 60 men to a carriage.

Later that year Camp Commandant Calcaterra and the guard who shot Socks were both killed by Italian partisans.

Christmas Booklet from the Pope to all Allied POWs in Italy for Christmas 1942

STALAG IV-B IN GERMANY

The train set off from Udine station and travelled up through the Alps into Austria. As the train slowed on the steep gradient and the night fell a lot of wagon doors were forced open and out went several of the lads. Each wagon had two guards on a small platform at the back and as the night wore on they took quick shots at fleeting figures in the dark.

STALAG XVIII-A WOLFSBERG

Stalag XVIII-A was a Second World War German Army (Wehrmacht) Prisoner of War (POW) camp located to the south of the town of Wolfsberg, in the southern Austrian state of Carinthia, then a part of Nazi Germany. Stalag is an abbreviation of the German Stammlager (Main Camp). A sub-camp Stalag XVIII-A/Z was later opened in Spittal an der Drau about 100 km (62 mi) to the west.

The camp, first designated Oflag XVIII-B, was opened at the site of a former parade ground on 19 October 1939, after the German invasion of Poland. The first inmates were Polish officers, from Spring 1940 also Belgian and French officers captured in the Battle of France. Wolfsberg remained a sub-camp of Stalag

XVII-A Kaisersteinbruch, until in March 1941 the officers were transferred to other camps and the camp was redesignated a Stalag of the military district XVIII, with French and Belgian prisoners being transferred in from Stalag XVII-A. The first British and Commonwealth prisoners arrived in July 1941 from a transit camp in Thessaloniki, Greece, having been captured during the battles of Greece and Crete. The first Soviet prisoners arrived in October 1941, and were housed in a separate enclosure.

In December a typhus epidemic broke out, and the entire camp was quarantined until March 1942. Many prisoners died, mainly Russians, as their living conditions and rations were substantially inferior to the other prisoners. In June 1942, to ease overcrowding, three new barracks were built, and 400 British NCOs were transferred to Stalag XVIII-B at Spittal. In January 1943 the camp at Spittal became a Zweiglager (sub-camp) of Wolfsberg, and was redesignated as Stalag XVIII-A/Z. In March 1943 a Lazarett (Camp Hospital) was built there.

In November 1943, after the Italian armistice, Italian and Commonwealth prisoners arrived from Italy. Two hundred NCOs were transferred to Stalag XVIII-C at Markt-Pongau in June 1944. That month there were a total of 38,831 prisoners registered at the camp. Of these 10,667 were British and Commonwealth troops, of which only 825 were in the main camp, while the rest were attached to various Arbeitskommandos (Labour Units). In August 1944, according to a Red Cross report, there were 313 Arbeitskommandos attached to Stalag XVIII-A, which were split fairly equally between Landwirtschaft (agriculture or forestry) and Gewerbliche Wirtschaft (trade and industry). There were several attempts to escape, primarily from the Arbeitskommandos.

On 18 December 1944 the camp was bombed by US aircraft. Forty-six prisoners and several guards were killed. Both the British and French camp hospitals were hit, with the British hut being almost completely destroyed. On the approach of Allied forces in April 1945 all fit prisoners from the camps and neighbouring labour units were marched east to Stalag XVIII-C.

Officially, the camp was liberated by elements of the British 8th Army on 11 May 1945. In fact the prisoners had been in control of the camp since the 8th, the day of the German surrender. That day the Kommandant, Hauptmann Steiner, had handed over control of the camp to the Senior British Medical Officer and the 'Men of Confidence'. French and British prisoners disarmed their guards and took control of the camp armoury, and the local Post Office, Railway Station and Police Station. Over the next few weeks the prisoners were transported via Klagenfurt to transit camps in Bari and Naples, from where they were eventually repatriated. By the middle of June only Russian prisoners remained, these were eventually exchanged for Allied POWs in Russian hands, near Graz. The camp then served as a British detention centre for ex-Nazis, before finally closing in mid-1947.

The next day the train stopped and the remaining POWs were moved temporarily into Stalag XVIII-A/Z at Spittal and Wolfsberg in Austria. Jack recalls that it contained British soldiers captured in Greece and Crete. He also recalls that they seem to have it pretty good. He noticed that their boots were polished and their buttons were shined. The inhabitants of Stalag XVIII-A/Z looked on the 'Colonials' as wretched intruders. They were kept in one area and mixing was discouraged. The visitors were fed a vegetable broth and given a loaf of bread between seven men. They slept in empty huts but the inhabitants refused to let them use the shower block. The visitors spent a few days in Stalag XVIII-A/Z and the menu was the same every day. Soon these liquid meals were called 'skilly' as shorthand to avoid referring to the vegetable of the day—cabbage, sugar beets, pickles, cauliflower, millet, beans, sauerkraut. Some found the food so monotonous or distasteful that they didn't eat and many—including Jack—would then return for a second serve.

After a miserable week in Stalag XVIII-A/Z on 24 September 1943 the visitors were put back into the carriages and resumed their journey. No one knew where they were going. Jack noticed that at night there was no blackout in effect so they concluded that they were out of range of the Allied bombers. For ten long days they travelled further and further north into Germany. The train was stopped periodically to let the POWs to urinate and defecate. If a tap was available at the stop they would try to have a quick wash. They were fed a skilly at lunch and given a loaf between seven men at night. Without realising the significance of the station they had to stop at Dachau outside Munich for two days because of air raids. The POWs noticed a 'sickly' smell in the air and had wide ranging discussions on what it could be. They also noticed that at times some form of masking scent was also noticeable—perhaps an attempt by the Germans to hide the grisly actions that were under way.

Prisoner of War Number 225687

Finally the journey ended and they arrived at Muhlberg and moved into a new camp called Stalag IV-B. Muhlberg is about 110 kilometres south of Berlin, 50 kilometres east of Leipzig and 40 kilometres north-west of Dresden. Stalag IV-B was run by the Wehrmacht—the German Army.

All the prisoners were processed into the German system and Jack was assigned POW Number 225687. He was issued a metal tag with his POW number stamped on it to be worn around

STALAG IV-B MÜHLBERG

Stalag IV-B was one of the largest Prisoner of War (POW) camps in Germany during the Second World War. Stalag is an abbreviation of the German Stammlager (Main Camp). Stalag IV-B was located 8 km (5.0 mi) north-east of the town of Mühlberg in the Prussian Province of Saxony, just east of the Elbe River and about 30 mi (48 km) north of Dresden.

The camp, covering about 30 hectares (74 acres), was opened in September 1939. The first inmates were about 17,000 Polish soldiers captured in the German September 1939 offensive. For the first two months they dwelt under the open sky or in tents. Most of them were transferred further to other camps.

In May 1940 the first French soldiers arrived, taken prisoner in the Battle of France. In 1941 British, and Australian soldiers arrived after the fall of Greece, and later in the year Russian POWs from the invasion of the Soviet Union. In September 1943, further numbers of British, Australian, New Zealand, and South African soldiers, previously captive in Italy, arrived after the Italian capitulation.

In October 1944 several thousand Poles arrived, members of the Armia Krajowa (Home Army) captured after the Warsaw Uprising, including several hundred women soldiers. In November 1944 the Polish women were transferred to other camps, mainly Stalag IV-E (Altenburg) and Oflag IX-C (Molsdorf). At the end of December 1944 about 7,500 Americans arrived from the Battle of the Bulge. At least 3,000 of them were transferred to other camps, mostly to Stalag VIII-A.

On 23 April 1945 the Red Army liberated the camp. Altogether soldiers from 33 nations passed through the camp. When the Soviet Army arrived at the camp in

April 1945, there were about 30,000 crowded into the facilities, of these 7,250 were British. It is estimated that between 1939 and 1945 approximately 300,000 prisoners from over 40 nations passed through the camp. About 3,000 died, mainly from tuberculosis and typhus. They were buried in the cemetery in neighbouring Neuburxdorf, Bad Liebenwerda. Today a memorial and a museum commemorate them.

The Soviet liberators held the British and American prisoners in the camp for over a month. Individual soldiers 'escaped' from the camp and made their way on foot to the American lines.

In August 1945 the Soviet secret police NKVD opened on the area of Stalag IV-B one of its special camps No. 1 using the shacks of Stalag IV-B. More than 22,800 persons were imprisoned and over 6,700 of them died until operation of the camp was ceased in 1948.

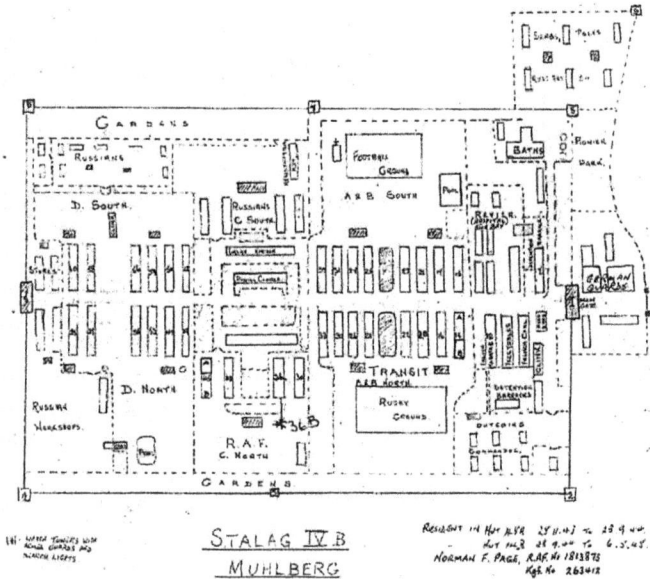

The Stalag IV-B Layout

The Front Gate to Stalag IV-B

The main street at Stalag IV-B

A guard tower at Stalag IV-B

The ablution and shower block at Stalag IV-B

Washing drying on the wire at Stalag IV-B

his neck. As the camp was still being constructed the prisoners were housed in six man tents erected on the parade ground. They were issued with jackets, three coarse blankets and straw but the approaching winter made staying warm challenging. In the midst of winter they were eventually moved into the completed wooden huts. Each was 30 metres long and 10 metres wide and housed about 200-220 men. The building was divided into units; each with two three tier bunks beds. Jack got a lower bunk—the worst of the three options. Each bunk was fitted with 14 boards—which tended to disappear over time.

The huts each had a stove with a solid iron hotplate on which the POWs could heat water, toast the ersatz bread and generally make food more palatable. Keeping the stoves alight during the winter was a challenge given the lack of fuel. Jack's hut had a 'big Kiwi Sergeant pilot' who organised raids for firewood. In early 1944 Jack recalls a raiding party stole all the posts from the barbed wire fence that separated one compound from the next. As the fence was 120 feet long this was no easy feat and demanded military planning and precision execution. The team was assigned specific tasks, tools were prepared, the Russians in the adjacent compound were co-opted, the fence was rolled up, moved, cut up and hidden in various locations all within a matter of hours on a Sunday when the guard numbers were reduced. And suffice that it provided a good source of firewood for some time.

The Army POWs in the next compound protested as, it was later revealed, they were digging a tunnel and didn't want to attract the attention of the 'goons'. The German NCO—Corporal Schmidt who had lost part of his left arm at the Russian Front—came into the compound on Monday morning for roll call and didn't notice until it was time for him to leave. The look of disbelief on his face was priceless. Corporal Schmidt then stormed off and returned with a padlock which he used to close the gate between two sections of the compound. Within seconds the lock had been picked and the POWs called out to Corporal Schmidt. He saw that his efforts were in vain, started to draw his pistol but then threw his hands in the air and stormed out of the compound. Corporal Schmidt got some revenge days later with a roll call in the middle of a cold night. Sadly, the tunnel was discovered by the Germans a few weeks later when a farmer's tractor collapsed one section.

The Germans realised that the wood around the camp was disappearing so they started to distribute a coal ration to each hut. Needless to say this was not enough and then coal raids became the activity of the day. The coal hut was located in a neighbouring compound for British Army troops. Jack's hut constructed a coal box out of a Canadian Red Cross parcel box lined with bed boards and fitted with handles. Teams of four carriers were identified and practiced relaying with other teams because of the weight. These hefty lads were also tasked with lifting the metal doors of the coal hut off their hinges—thus bypassing the chain and padlock. A network of lookouts or 'cockatoos'—including Jack—was formed and trained. Others were assigned as shovellers with orders to remove coal from the back of the pile and not the front. A coal raid was mounted every night which would secure enough coal for the stove to run for the next 24 hours. In addition to the hazard of running into guards and spotlights was the chance of coincidentally running into the raiding team from another hut. Jack recalls that the Germans got really upset with the occupants of the hut next to the coal hut who they assumed must be responsible for the thefts.

One effort to secure coal, however, ended in tragic circumstances. Sergeant 'Taffy' Jones—a RAF rear gunner—began a habit of stealing out of his barracks in the early morning to grab some coal briquettes through a loose brick in the corner of the coal hut. This method worked well for several weeks—much to the appreciation of his hut mates—but one morning he was surprised by a German shepherd guard dog and then shot by a sentry. The sentry laid Taffy's sack over his head and he was left there for all the camp to see at morning roll call.

Another method to secure coal later in the war was to illegally 'buy' it from the German guards. The demand for coal triggered a supply line that went all the way back through the compound guards, the gate guards, the truck drivers and the mine managers. The exchange rate was 10 cigarettes per hundredweight but it was 'best' to buy a ton at a time for 200 cigarettes. The cigarettes came in the Red Cross parcels. Since many POWs didn't smoke it became common for large piles of coal to be inside each hut. The arrangement worked well for all parties, but occasionally the Gestapo got involved trying to identify which guards were part of this black market and would typically confiscate all the coal from the huts as 'punishment'.

Jack observed that while the more senior German guards were 'officious' many of the lower ranks were older, sometimes infirm and pretty ambivalent about things. Picking up the POWs for infractions of the rules just meant more paperwork. Many of them were corruptible and just looking to survive the war. Often they would be given gifts of cigarettes, coffee or condensed milk simply to be in a compromising position that could be leveraged at a later date. As the war progressed and Germany came under increasing pressure the guards became even more apathetic and pliable.

The prisoners were issued more food than in Italy but a lot of it was old and rotten. Potatoes featured in the rations and they were stored in deep pits lined with straw. Other vegetables such as coarse millet, sugar beet, turnips and cabbage were usually turned into a broth. Flour often contained maggots. Any meat that arrived was usually more bone than meat but it at least added some flavour to the broth. Jack recalls once when six horse heads arrived; the cooks simply smashed them with axes and boiled them in a cauldron before drawing off the liquid to mix with the broth. As in Italy, the Red Cross parcels provided much needed food and other essential items.

The Germans allowed the POWs to use one of the huts as a theatre and several groups formed to produce musicals and plays—sometimes being performed on a weekly basis. One play—the Man Who Came to Dinner—was so popular it ran for several weeks. Some of the POWs were excellent female impersonators and others discovered their natural talent for acting and comedy.

There were other characters. Jack recalls one fellow in particular—Bill Rae. Bill was a Scottish Jew who was captured in Greece in early 1942. Whenever he was involved or associated with an escape Bill was interrogated and tortured with electric probes. Several of his toes were cut off with bolt cutters. Bill never 'ratted' on his mates and was stoic throughout his suffering. Back in the compound, Jack remembers him always laughing and making jokes around the camp.

'Skilling Up' for a meal. Judging by 'the look' probably sugar beet or sauerkraut

French POWs receiving Red Cross Parcels. Each tin was 'spiked' open so that it couldn't be kept for future escapes

Production of The Man who came to Dinner. Note the six 'women' on stage and the orchestra

In addition to plays and musicals the POWs ran lectures and also produced newspapers and magazines. *Flywheel* was a hand drawn newsletter produced by members of the 'Muhlberg Motor Club' within Stalag IV-B. The newsletter was founded by Tom Swallow, and comprised pages from school exercise-books that carried hand-written articles with colour illustrations from whatever inks the editorial team could produce from stolen materials, like quinine from the medical room; these were stuck into place with fermented millet soup, kept from the meagre camp rations.

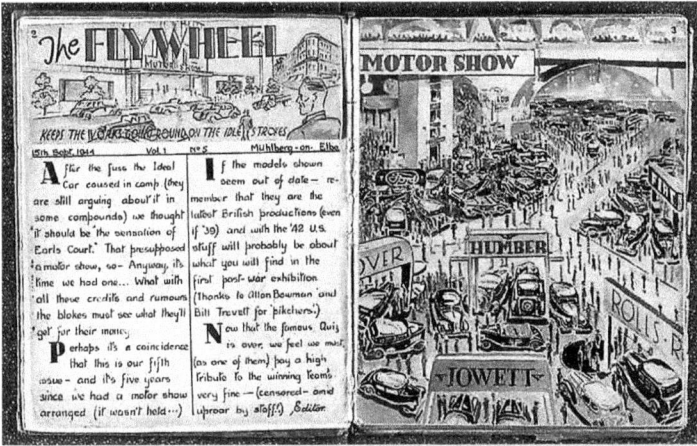

A sample from Flywheel magazine

One copy per issue was produced, to be circulated among members throughout the camp. Ten newsletters were produced covering topics such as motoring adventures before the war, road tests of cars and motor cycles, a speculative 1944 motor show, advertisements, editorial comment and even a letters page nostalgically reflecting pre-war life. Bikes and cars that were no longer produced, but with names that are legend were all recalled. The pages were filled with drawings and sketches that are both graphic and realistic, and text full of wit, enthusiasm and authority. Jack recalls that one issue encouraged readers to design the ultimate motor vehicle generated weeks of heated debate around the camp. When extracts from *Flywheel* were published in a book in 1987 it ran to two reprints; capturing the imagination of a new readership as well as reminding many old soldiers of the privations suffered at German hands.

On Anzac Day 1944 the Germans allowed the Australians and New Zealanders to have a parade. The Camp Commandant took the salute as the contingent marched along the main street. Being permitted to march and participate in a bit of national commemoration was a significant privilege that was warmly received by the Anzac POWs—even though there was no opportunity to have a drink or play two-up.

Anzac Day Parade 1944

In early April 1944, no doubt with the aim of impressing the RAAF POWs, two German pilots in twin-engine Junkers 88s from nearby Lonnewitz airfield, flew over the camp. This went on for two to three weeks and sometimes up to three times a day. The heights reduced with every pass until the aircraft were only about 20 to 30 feet above ground. Different approaches to the camp were taken and then combined with increasingly dangerous acrobatic manoeuvres. One day, the POWs were holding a football match and several thousand POWs were watching.

A Junkers 88

POWs lying down after a low pass by a Junkers 88 at Stalag IV-B

The German pilot swooped down to just clear the heads of the crowd at one touchline, lowered the aircraft to just a few feet above the pitch and then pulling up just in time to clear the crowd at the other touchline. The camp leaders lodged a protest with the Camp Commandant at this dangerous behaviour. However, the behaviour didn't stop and a week later on 30 April 1944 one of the aircraft zoomed down one of the clear areas between the huts and the wire. The pilot realised he was in trouble at one point and pulled up sharply. Unfortunately, the tail plane dropped and hit two prisoners who were walking along the wire. Sergeant Herb Mallory was decapitated and Sergeant Wally Massie was seriously injured. Sergeant Mallory was later buried with full military honours at the local cemetery. Justice was done however as a camp guard later revealed that the pilot had been court martialled, stripped of his rank, sent to gaol and on release would be posted as an infantry private to a battalion on the Russian front.

The POWs could see and sense the growing Allied air offensive against Germany. US Air Force Bombers could be observed flying overhead during the day and at night red glowing fires could be seen in the cities of Berlin, Leipzig and Dresden. Often parachutes could be seen as crew members escaped damaged aircraft. Once a crew member landed heavily in the fields outside the camp. When the guards brought the airman into the camp the POWs tried to communicate with him but he refused to say anything other than his name, rank and serial number. They learned after a couple of days that the airman thought he had been brought into a 'fake' POW camp and that the POWs were Germans pretending to be POWs in order to get information from him. As it turned out the Germans had established such a facility (but not on the scale of Stalag IV-B) and the airman had been briefed to be wary of such a set up.

On another occasion a formation of US 'Flying Fortress' heavy bombers passed so low that they could make out the 'gunships' amongst them; these were aircraft that carried no bombs and fitted with extra guns. The gunships flew at the back of the main formation and if a German fighter approached they would manoeuvre quickly and poured a tremendous amount of firepower at them. Throughout 1944 the Allies increasingly commanded the skies above Germany. And while the boost to morale was tremendous the number of POWs—especially American aircrew as well as American soldiers captured during the Battle of the Bulge—in the camp increased by thousands to the point of overcrowding; creating food shortages, sanitation problems and outbreaks of dysentery, diphtheria and several forms of respiratory infections. Trips to the delousing showers became more regular.

Towards the end of 1944 a large number of Polish women and children moved through the camp—albeit in a different compound. Some of the POWs could speak Polish and soon learned that they were being moved from the Warsaw ghetto after the uprising. Almost all of them were moved on to other camps and some met a fateful end. One Australian POW who was helping out became friendly enough to slip a girl his address in Australia was able to re-kindle the friendship after the war and eventually they were married. Their response at dinner parties of the question 'So, how did you two meet?' was sure to receive looks of astonishment.

By the end of 1944 the mood amongst the POWs was beginning to lift. It was likely that this would be their last winter in prison. Each new inmate and BBC reports brought news and tracking the ever-moving 'front-line' on a map became a popular activity. Rumours swirled and debate raged on the relative merits of Montgomery and Patton on the German border in the west. But the front with the most significance lay to the east. By the

Model of Stalag IV-B built by a French POW

end of 1944 the massive Russian Army was advancing through Poland and at the gates of Warsaw. The approaching winter was likely to witness a new Russian offensive.

At Christmas the Germans allowed the POWs to sing not only Christmas carols but also 'patriotic' songs. German officers joined the POWs at services in the Recreation Hut and a reflective mood seemed to take hold across the camp. Red Cross parcels became more sporadic as the Allied air offensive started to really bite into the German logistics systems.

In the closing months of the war another remarkable activity occurred within Stalag IV-B. Mrs Florence Barrington—a British subject—was married to a German and living in Vienna in 1939. Her son—Winston—from an earlier marriage had returned to England at the outbreak of the war and joined the RAF. Winston was shot down and interred at Stalag IV-B. When his mother discovered this she moved to the area and convinced the Commandant to allow her to visit her son periodically. As the Eastern Front moved closer and the Allied bombing intensified Winston was concerned for his mother's safety. He managed to smuggle her into the camp where she remained hidden in plain sight amongst the growing number of POWs until war's end. Not surprisingly, very few of the POWs knew about this and many never learned of it until many years after the war.

As expected the Russians launched their 'Vistula-Oder' offensive in January 1945. Within a matter of days the Red Army advanced hundreds of kilometres, taking much of Poland and striking deep within the pre-war borders of the Reich. The offensive broke the German Army Group A, and much of Germany's remaining capacity for military resistance. On 27 January 1945 Russian troops liberated the Auschwitz concentration camp. Despite attempts by retreating SS units to destroy parts of the camp, the Soviet forces still found graphic evidence of the Holocaust.

On 31 January 1945, the Soviet offensive was voluntarily halted, though Berlin was undefended and only approximately 70 km away from the Soviet bridgeheads across the Oder River. The Vistula-Oder offensive was followed by a period of several weeks of mopping-up and consolidation on the part of the Red Army, along with ongoing hard fighting in pockets in the north.

Throughout January 1945, the SS and Nazi-controlled police units had begun forcing thousands of POWs in Poland, East Prussia, Silesia and Pomerania to walk westward away from the advancing Red Army. The death marches, which took place over hundreds of kilometres in sub-zero conditions without food and medicine, resulted in thousands of concentration camp prisoners and allied POWs dying on route. It is estimated that in March and April 1945 at least 250,000 men and women were marched on foot to the heartland of Germany and Austria sometimes for weeks at a time.

On 16 April 1945 the Red Army jumped off from lines on the Oder and Neisse Rivers, the opening phase of the Battle of Berlin, which proved to be the culminating offensive of the war on the Eastern Front. The outcome of the war was certain and liberation at Stalag IV-B seemed only a matter of weeks or even days away.

The German guards were either trying to ingratiate themselves with the POWs or making plans to get away from the Russians—or both. Roll calls became a farce and no more than an exercise in justifying the ration draw. Jimmy Edwards who worked as the camp's Australian Postal Officer 'liberated' the files on the camps inmates. Sweepstakes were started to predict the liberation date. 10 cigarettes was the minimum bet. Jack bet on a day in June—and as it turned out he was miles off.

At about 10 am on 24 April 1945 Russian soldiers appeared at the gates of Stalag IV-B. The happy sweepstake winner pocketed over 1,000 cigarettes. The Red Army officer was mounted on a pony and

SOVIET OFFENSIVE IN GERMANY
APRIL-MAY 1945

The Soviet offensive had two objectives. Because of Stalin's suspicions about the intentions of the Western Allies to hand over territory occupied by them in the post-war Soviet sphere of influence, the offensive was to be on a broad front and was to move as rapidly as possible to the west, to meet the Western Allies as far west as possible. But the overriding objective was to capture Berlin. The two were complementary because possession of the zone could not be won quickly unless Berlin was taken. Another consideration was that Berlin itself held strategic assets, including Adolf Hitler and part of the German atomic bomb program.

The offensive to capture central Germany and Berlin started on 16 April 1945 with an assault on the German front lines on the Oder and Neisse rivers. After several days of heavy fighting the Soviet 1st Belorussian Front and 1st Ukrainian Front punched holes through the German front line and were fanning out across central Germany. By 24 April 1945, elements of the 1st Belorussian Front and 1st Ukrainian Front had completed the encirclement of the German capital and the Battle of Berlin entered its final stages.

On 25 April 1945 the 2nd Belorussian Front broke through the German 3rd Panzer Army's line south of Stettin. The Soviets were now free to move west towards the British 21st Army Group and north towards the Baltic port of Stralsund. The 58th Guards Rifle Division of the 5th Guards Army made contact with the US 69th Infantry Division of the First Army near Torgau, Germany at the Elbe River.

On 29 and 30 April 1945, as the Soviet forces fought their way into the centre of Berlin, Adolf Hitler married

Eva Braun and then committed suicide by taking cyanide and shooting himself. Helmuth Weidling, defence commandant of Berlin, surrendered the city to the Soviet forces on 2 May 1945. On 7 May 1945, at SHAEF headquarters, German Chief-of-Staff General Alfred Jodl signed the unconditional surrender documents for all German forces to the Allies at Reims in France.

apparently the leading armoured troops had advanced past the prison the previous night. The camp inmates learned that day that the Camp Commandant had made a well-timed departure several hours beforehand but had as a matter of courtesy met with the senior Allied officer and 'man of confidence'—Major Little—and informed him of their intention to depart, transferred responsibility for administration of the POWs and wished 'us' all the best. For the thousands of POWs in Stalag IV-B's the war was essentially over, but the challenges were not yet finished.

LIBERATION

As the POWs milled about the camp and wondered what would happen next, Jack and a couple of his mates—Sandy Mostran and Jimmy Edwards—posed for a rare photo to record the occasion. Jimmy Edwards had liberated a camera from the fleeing Germans and agreed to sell it to an English POW for 50 cigarettes. There was one exposure left in the camera and so in appreciation of the sale the Englishman snapped a photo of the three mates in front of the toilet block. Jack would not get to see that photo for another 50 years. And little did the three of them realise that they would pose for similar photos decades later.

Sandy Mostran, Jack Bell and Jimmy Edwards

The former Hitler Youth barracks in Riesa

The Russians warned the POWs that 'mopping up' operations were still underway and that the safest thing to do was stay in the camp. The Russians allowed them to eat as much of the ration store as they wanted. Jack and Sandy Jones grabbed an armful of rhubarb which they stewed up and gorged far too quickly. After years existing on half-a ladle of food a day they should have known better but both suffered from severe diarrhoea the next day.

It was supposed to be liberation, but the Russians seemed in no mood for celebrations. When the initial euphoria wore off the POWs started to sense that maybe they had been re-captured and had just swapped one lot of captors for another. As it turns out there was an element of truth in this sense as the Russians regarded Allied POWs as useful leverage as the war in Europe reached its conclusion. The challenge in communicating with the Russians added to the sense of uncertainty and foreboding.

Although the POWs didn't realise it at the time the Allies had agreed that the Elbe River was to form the boundary between the US advance from the west and the Russian advance from the east. Muhlberg and Stalag IV-B were located on the eastern side of the Elbe River and so the camp was liberated by the Russians. But the US Army was only a few kilometres away.

After three days—on Victory in Europe Day—the Russians ordered them to get ready to depart the camp. Hopes soared for passage towards the American lines, but the more sinister options were the subject of fierce rumours. Arriving at a former Hitler Youth barracks near Riesa, Jack and Sandy Jones and a few others decided they would set up in a vacant cookhouse, complete with large vat cookers full of some cold brown 'stew-like' substance that even they weren't brave enough to eat.

Foraging nearby for food in an eerily quiet village they group discovered a case of Hennessy Brandy amongst a pile of rubbish. Its owner—a German grocer—stared angrily down at them from a first floor window. Just then two Russian soldiers walked past with a case of some type of tinned meat and with the use of sign language six bottles of Brandy were traded for 12 tins of meat. Back at the German cookhouse the group agreed that opening one bottle and having a small sip was the prudent thing to do. One sip led to another and before long they were all quite inebriated. Jack was later informed that he wandered up to some Russians working in a repair shop and abused them before being led away by his mates. He protested vigorously and broke away to collapse a short distance away. When Jack woke several hours later it took him some time to make his way back to the cookhouse in the dark.

The next day the group met up with a Russian intelligence officer who told them that the US and Russian Armies had met up on the Elbe River. Communicating was a challenge and at one point the group feared the Russian believed they were German soldiers. The Russian had never heard of Australia and so they had to tell him that they were British. They learned that soldiers from the two armies were not permitted to fraternise, but that refugees and POWs were being allowed to cross the River on a temporary bridge. Deciding to take their fate into their own hands the group 'headed off' that afternoon. As they walked west the occasional sound of gunfire and explosions caused some consternation—mopping up was indeed still underway.

The group camped overnight in a farmhouse and befriending an old man and the women at the farm the group enjoyed a supper of cheese, potatoes and fresh milk. The farmers asked if the group could do anything about the Russians coming and stealing all their food and milk; and sadly they replied that they could not. Heading off early the next morning the group increasingly came across Russian soldiers who were friendly and were happy to provide directions. At one time they even received a lift in a truck which was carrying wounded. The front line troops seemed more professional and disciplined than the rear echelon types.

Arriving at the eastern end of the bridge across the Elbe River the group presented themselves to a well-dressed US Army military policeman. After explaining who they were and their situation the Military Policeman simply said 'Go!' At the western end of the bridge another US Military Policeman came to them and led them to a nearby camp. It was about three or four o'clock in the afternoon but they were taken straight to the mess tent and served a meal immediately. This time, Jack ate sparingly but the rations tasted like heaven. It was 15 May 1945 and now it really felt as though their war was over.

After a meal each member of the group was interviewed to get their details. The group was then informed that they would be flown to Brussels the next day. They were given a K ration and some chocolate bars and settled in for their first night's sleep in freedom. The next morning the group boarded a DC2 transport aircraft and on arrival in Brussels were greeted warmly by Red Cross personnel who served them tea and coffee and slices of freshly baked white bread which Jack recalls tasted like cake.

They were billeted in a hut and told that they would be flown to England the next day. Jack and Sandy Jones went for a bit of a wander around Brussels and called in on the Australian Army Liaison Officer in a building on the town square. Jack and Sandy were not too impressed with him but were feeling sufficiently chirpy about their situation that they gifted the senior officer their last bottle of brandy from Reisa. To this day Jack regrets giving away that bottle.

On the 18 May 1945 a group of POWs were flown back to England on a Lancaster bomber. For many of the passengers this was their first encounter with this magnificent aircraft. When they arrived at the RAF base they were taken to a delousing section and told to strip off all their clothes. Jack was loathe to give up the bomber jacket he had been shot down in and had worn throughout his captivity but despite his pleadings to the delousing staff, they would not give it back to him. After washing they were transported to Brighton and kitted out in brand new RAAF uniforms—including helmet and gas mask.

Each POW was then individually debriefed. Jack's interviewing officer was Squadron Leader Eddie Broad, the younger brother of Jack Broad. Jack had known Jack Broad since child hood and had shown him around the camp in Cairo back in 1941, but sadly he was later killed. On his debrief questionnaire Jack wrote in response to the question describe events immediately prior to and leading up to capture—'Crash landed in flames in midst of 15th Panzer Division. Evacuated aircraft. Collapsed 100 ft from A/C [aircraft]. Captured'. Jack also provided details on what he thought happened to the others that were captured with him and any information he had about them after capture. The questionnaire also asked for figures on the number of Red Cross parcels received at each camp and Jack indicated that he had also received five clothing parcels from Australia.

As part of the interview each former-POW was also asked to give details of any war crimes they believe they had witnessed. Most POWs had a least one report to make and these were later cross-referenced

Australian former-POWs from Europe returning home on the SS Orion

Members of the crowd cheering as buses carrying Australian former-POWs, who have just disembarked from SS Orion, move off from Wooloomooloo wharf on their way to recruit reception and general details depot at Sydney showground

to provide evidence for war crimes trials. In Jack's debrief he reported that he witnessed Private Symonds being shot by a guard at Campo 57 in 1943.

Interviews complete they were then granted leave and allowed to draw down on their backlogged pay. Jack thought 10 pounds would see him through the week. The pay officer said 'Alright. I'll see you again tomorrow.' Jack enjoyed a beautiful meal near the Palladium Theatre—oysters, fish and apple pudding. It cost him 9 pounds so he was back to visit the pay officer again the next day. After three weeks of good food—and the occasional beer—Jack regained 42 pounds in 3 weeks. Staying at the RAAF Hotel they were given double rations. Breakfast consisted of cereal or porridge, 4 eggs and 6 rashes of bacon, toast, marmalade or jam, and as much milk as you wanted. This ration was way more than what was available to civilians.

On one trip to London he looked up D.&W. Murray Ltd in Great Portland Street. The staff were wonderful towards him and the managing director—John Hewitt—'paid' Jack 10 pounds each week for 'expenses' and also an escort—an older chap—to show him around. At times Jack was allowed access to the company car and driven around by a girl names Peggy—John Hewitt's secretary. In return Jack purchased items from the Red Cross to give to his hosts. With a free rein, Jack took the opportunity to visit Ireland and visit relatives including his mother's cousin—George Kincade. Arriving in Belfast Jack recalls seeing rows of German U-Boats in port. In shops and bars the returning POWs were often identified because of their brand new uniforms and given preferential treatment. Being an unassuming person, Jack recalls one episode in a fish shop where he was treated so well he felt particularly overwhelmed.

Late in July 1945 Jack and about 4,000 former-POWs boarded the SS *Orion* and departed London for Sydney via the Panama Canal. Crossing the Atlantic Jack recalls moving through one particularly bad storm where the bow rose and fell 30-40 feet and almost every passenger was sea sick. Sitting in the hold was not a pleasant experience. Crossing the Pacific Ocean news of the Japan's surrender came through on 15 August 1945. But because there was a fear of Japanese submarines that might not have been told to surrender they continued the voyage in blackout conditions. Berthing in Wellington for 24 hours Jack caught up with Alby Jack who was a former-POW that had been repatriated from Italy. Alby Jack's nickname was 'crow' for his habit of sitting on the sideline of a cricket match and offering his 'advice' on what the players should do. On 9 September 1945 the SS *Orion* arrived in Sydney.

A LIFE WORTH LIVING

O ne of the first things that Jack did after arriving in Sydney was to visit Tony Carter's mother. Tony was Jack's best friend having met on the EATS course and then travelled together in the same cabin to the Middle East. Tony was killed in the seat next to Jack when their aircraft was shot down in 1942. Jack recalls this as the hardest thing he has ever had to do, seeing the look in her eyes saying 'why my son and not you?' It was a very emotional, tearful and uncomfortable meeting but Jack felt a strong obligation to do this personally.

Jack then caught the train from Sydney up to Brisbane where the returning service-men were housed in the Sandgate camp. There he began his military discharge procedure but luckily was not far from home so was able to see his family quicker than others. Part of the discharge process was receiving his back pay—several hundred pounds. Another part was getting a medical assessment at a depot in Southport. There the doctors decided that he needed a full internal examination of his abdomen to make sure that things were well enough for him to be discharged. Awaiting exploratory surgery and taking advantage of the 'rules' he managed to have the RAAF train him up to Townsville for a week to visit some of his mother's relatives. Returning to Brisbane

Jack was operated on by Dr Sutton—a friend of his father's—and after a bit of 'tidying-up' was declared sufficiently fit for discharge. Again the several small pieces of shrapnel were left in his arm on the expectation that they would 'work themselves out over time' and again the doctors were wrong—two pieces remain to this day.

Jack was formally discharged from the RAAF on 25 January 1946. His final pay was seven pounds salary, 109 pounds in lieu of 137 days of accrued leave and an additional 20 pounds subsistence allowance. In recognition of Jacks service during the war he was awarded the 1939-45 Star, the Africa Star, the War Medal 1939-45, the Australian Service Medal 1939-1945 and the Returned from Active Service Badge.

The 'advice' for family members was to not talk to returning POWs about their experiences. This 'policy' might have been driven primarily by the terrible experience of those POWs in Japanese custody, but the net effect was that former POWs were encouraged to 'put things behind them' and 'buried' their feelings. This approach most probably had a negative effect on the mental health of former POWs and ex-servicemen and women over the next several decades. What we now refer to as Post-Traumatic Stress Disorder was then called 'anxiety'.

Presenting himself at the Sandgate sub-branch of the Returned and Services League Jack was coolly received by the few remaining members— almost all First World War veterans. Told to put his name on a waiting list for membership it would be another four years before Jack would end up joining the RSL in Melbourne; but even then he was a rare visitor to the sub-branch.

A number of unit associations for returned servicepersons formed after the war. But for RAAF members who had served in the UK, Europe and the Middle East in non-RAAF units there was no unit association for them to join. The 'Odd Bods' Association was formed in 1947 so that they could hold reunions and to remember those who had lost their lives during the war. Jack only joined the Odd Bods in the early 1980s. Cleverly he paid $50 to become a life member and has certainly gotten his money's worth nearly 40 years later.

Jack returned to Brisbane in February 1946 to try and take up his old job at D.&W. Murray Ltd. The manager he spoke to said they were only going to give him a job because they were legally required to—not in appreciation for your service. Two weeks later Jack took up the position of Manager in the Men's and Boy's Clothing Department. That manager was later relocated to Sydney as he had given short shrift to all the retuning servicemen.

In 1949 Jack was offered and accepted the position as the Sales Manager for the North-Western Woollen Mills in Stawell, Victoria. The wool industry was booming and the Mill was experiencing period of growth—and was operating three shifts a day. Jack was based in Melbourne at the company's office in Flinders Lane in Melbourne. Jack had a few pieces of memorabilia including his uniforms and POW dog tags (a metal badge on a cord) from his war service and stored it in his parents' house in Sandgate. Sadly, they were lost during a king tide in 1952.

The North Western Woollen Mills

*Jack looking pleased with himself
at the wedding in 1954*

Mr and Mrs Bell out for dinner 1954

In the Flinders Lane office was a young lady named Dolores Cook—the only daughter of Mr and Mrs G.W. Cook of Elsternwick. Dolores thought Jack was 'a bit of a dish' and before long they were dating. Jack and Dolores announced their engagement on 15 October 1953 and were married on 28 May 1954.

Later in 1954 Jack took up a position with W.M. Hopkins and Son who were the agents for the North Western Woollen Mills in Sydney and Brisbane. He and Dolores relocated to Brisbane and then after a year they offered him the Sales Manager position in their Sydney office. Dolores became pregnant and went to live with her parents in Melbourne. Sandra was born in April 1955.

Jack, Dolores and Sandra then lived in Sydney until Dolores' mother fell ill and they were obliged in late 1956 to relocate to Melbourne in order to support her. The owner Mr Hopkins offered Jack a position in their Melbourne office but sadly not at a commensurate level. So, after moving back to Melbourne Jack took up a sales position with Comspring Fabrics. Within 12 months Jack moved across to

Jack, Sandra and Dolores in 1955

Charles Parsons Pty Ltd—a fabric wholesaler—and ended up staying with that firm for the next 21 years. As part of his duties Jack travelled around the world visiting France, Italy, Czechoslovakia, Spain, the United Kingdom, Ireland, Germany, Korea and Taiwan. On one of these trips Jack coincidentally met the Italian captain that he had worked with to evacuate Italian wounded from the captured Quetta Fort in Libya. The captain had seen out the rest of the war as a prisoner returned to his family business running a silk mill in Como, Italy.

On 13 June 1963 Jack, Dolores and Sandra moved into a new house at 49 Russell Street in Surrey Hills where Jack and Dolores continue to live comfortably and happily to this day. After retiring in 1978 Jack assisted several overseas mills in getting established and improving their sales.

Jack Bell in the early 1960's

In 1980 a robber stole Jack's medals and it took several years for a set of replacements to be made and presented to him. Sandra married Neil Foster in 1984 and over the coming years had three children—Georgina, Alex and Penny.

As a Victorian resident of many decades Jack has been a strong supporter of the Shrine of Remembrance, the Victorian ex-POWs Association and the Victorian Branch of the Returned and Services League of Australia. He has assisted both organisations with raising awareness and fundraising appeals for the veteran community. Jack joined the Returned and Services League of Australia RSL and has been an active member of the Camberwell City sub-branch. In 2014 the President of the Evans Head Memorial Aerodrome and Heritage Aviation Association asked Jack to become their Patron.

Jack and his granddaughter Penny helping with the Shrine of Remembrance's Poppy Appeal

In the 1980's Jack's family encouraged him to write about his war time experiences and the account he produced was a primary source for the material in this book. Since then Jack has been more comfortable in talking about his war time experiences—which has been beneficial both for him and the people who seek to understand the experience of war and captivity.

In 1995 the English chap who had snapped the photo of the three Aussies in Stalag IV-B published a story in a UK magazine asking if anyone could help to identify them. One of Jack's mates saw the article and passed advice on to him. Fifty years after it had been taken, Jack finally got to see that photograph.

Over the last several years Jack has participated in a number of re-unions and commemorative events. In recent years Jack and Dolores have volunteered in opportunity shops demonstrating their remarkable commitment to community service.

In 2014 Jack and Dolores celebrated their 60th wedding anniversary and on 20 December 2017 Jack celebrated his 100th birthday.

Jack and Dolores celebrate 60 years of marriage in 2014

Jack at the Commemoration for the 70th Anniversary of VE Day in France in 2015

Jack meeting Prince Charles in 2015

Marcus Fielding was born and raised in Melbourne. He joined the Australian Regular Army in 1983 and graduated from the Royal Military College Duntroon as a Lieutenant in 1986.

In the following decades of military service Marcus held a broad range of senior appointments in Army, defence and interagency organisations in a number of locations throughout Australia and overseas.

Marcus has participated in four operational deployments. In 1992 he directed operations to clear land mines in Afghanistan. In 1995 he coordinated infrastructure construction projects in Haiti.

In 1999 and 2000 Marcus directed security operations and coordinated the repatriation of displaced persons as part of the Australian-led international force in East Timor. For his work in East Timor, he was awarded a Commendation for Distinguished Service.

In 2008 and 2009 Marcus spent nine months in Baghdad as an 'action officer' in the Headquarters Multi-National Force–Iraq. In 2011 he published a book about his experiences in Iraq titled *Red Zone Baghdad*. Colonel Fielding transferred from full-time to part-time service with the Australian Army in 2011.

Marcus is the President of the Camberwell City Sub-Branch of the Returned and Services League of Australia and of President of Military History and Heritage Victoria—an inclusive forum for individuals and groups who are passionate about military history and heritage in Victoria.

www.ingramcontent.com/pod-product-compliance
Lightning Source LLC
Chambersburg PA
CBHW060813100426
42813CB00004B/1053